RISING INEQUALITY in the UNITED STATES

RISING INEQUALITY in the UNITED STATES

Armed Forces Implications and Governmental Policy Response

Pamela Ligouri Bunker
and Robert J. Bunker

A *Small Wars Journal* Pocket Book

To order additional copies of this book, contact:
Xlibris
1-888-795-4274
www.Xlibris.com
Orders@Xlibris.com
791342

CONTENTS

ABOUT SMALL WARS
JOURNAL AND FOUNDATION

Small Wars Journal facilitates the exchange of information among practitioners, thought leaders, and students of Small Wars, in order to advance knowledge and capabilities in the field. We hope this, in turn, advances the practice and effectiveness of those forces prosecuting Small Wars in the interest of self-determination, freedom, and prosperity for the population in the area of operations.

We believe that Small Wars are an enduring feature of modern politics. We do not believe that true effectiveness in Small Wars is a 'lesser included capability' of a force tailored for major theater war. And we *never* believed that 'bypass built-up areas' was a tenable position warranting the doctrinal primacy it has held for too long—this site is an evolution of the MOUT Homepage, Urban Operations Journal, and urbanoperations. com, all formerly run by the *Small Wars Journal's* Editor-in-Chief.

The characteristics of Small Wars have evolved since the Banana Wars and Gunboat Diplomacy. War is never purely military, but today's Small Wars are even less pure with the greater inter-connectedness of the 21st century. Their conduct typically involves the projection and employment of the full spectrum of national and coalition power by a broad community of practitioners. The military is still generally the biggest part of the pack, but there are a lot of other wolves. The strength of the pack is the wolf, and the strength of the wolf is the pack.

The *Small Wars Journal's* founders come from the Marine Corps. Like Marines deserve to be, we are very proud of this; we are also conscious and cautious of it. This site seeks to transcend any viewpoint that is single service, and any that is purely military or naively U.S.-centric. We pursue a comprehensive approach to Small Wars, integrating the full joint, allied, and coalition military with their governments' federal or national agencies, non-governmental agencies, and private organizations. Small Wars are big undertakings, demanding a coordinated effort from a huge community of interest.

We thank our contributors for sharing their knowledge and experience, and hope you will continue to join us as we build a resource for our community of interest to engage in a professional dialog on this painfully relevant topic. Share your thoughts, ideas, successes, and mistakes; make us all stronger.

"...I know it when I see it."

"Small Wars" is an imperfect term used to describe a broad spectrum of spirited continuation of politics by other means, falling somewhere in the middle bit of the continuum between feisty diplomatic words and global thermonuclear war. The *Small Wars Journal* embraces that imperfection.

Just as friendly fire isn't, there isn't necessarily anything small about a Small War.

The term "Small War" either encompasses or overlaps with a number of familiar terms such as counterinsurgency, foreign internal defense, support and stability operations, peacemaking, peacekeeping, and many flavors of intervention. Operations such as noncombatant evacuation, disaster relief, and humanitarian assistance will often either be a part of a Small War, or have a Small Wars feel to them. Small Wars involve a wide spectrum of specialized tactical, technical, social, and cultural skills and expertise, requiring great ingenuity from their practitioners. The *Small Wars Manual* (a wonderful resource, unfortunately more often referred to than read) notes that:

> *Small Wars demand the highest type of leadership directed by intelligence, resourcefulness, and ingenuity. Small Wars are conceived in uncertainty, are conducted often with precarious responsibility and doubtful authority, under indeterminate orders lacking specific instructions.*

The "three block war" construct employed by General Krulak is exceptionally useful in describing the tactical and operational challenges of a Small War and of many urban operations. Its only shortcoming is that is so useful that it is often mistaken as a definition or as a type of operation.

We'd like to deploy a primer on Small Wars that provides more depth than this brief section. Your suggestions and contributions of content are welcome.

Who Are Those Guys?

Small Wars Journal is NOT a government, official, or big corporate site. It is run by <u>Small Wars Foundation,</u> a non-profit corporation, for the benefit of the Small Wars community of interest. The site principals are Dave Dilegge (Editor-in-Chief) and Bill Nagle (Publisher), and it would not be possible without the support of myriad volunteers as well as authors who care about this field and contribute their original works to the community. We do this in our spare time, because we want to. McDonald's pays more. But we'd rather work to advance our noble profession than watch TV, try to super-size your order, or interest you in a delicious hot apple pie. If and when you're not flipping burgers, please join us.

Author Biographies

PAMELA LIGOURI BUNKER is a researcher and analyst specializing in international security and terrorism—with a narratives analytical focus—and is presently a non-resident fellow in terrorism and counterterrorism, TRENDS Research and Advisory, Abu Dhabi and an associate with *Small Wars Journal—El Centro*. She is a past senior officer of the Counter-OPFOR Corporation and has professional experience in research and program coordination in university, non-governmental organization (NGO), and city government settings. She holds undergraduate degrees in anthropology-geography and social sciences from California State Polytechnic University Pomona, an M.A. in public policy from the Claremont Graduate University, and an M.Litt. in terrorism studies from the University of Saint Andrews, Scotland. She is co-author of the Terrorism Research Center eBook *The Islamic State English-Language Online Magazine Rumiyah (Rome): Research Guide, Narrative & Threat Analysis and U.S. Policy Response* (2019), editor of the *SWJ Plutocratic Insurgency Reader* (2019), co-author of the SSI USAWC book *Radical Islamist English-Language Online Magazines: Research Guide, Strategic Insights, and Policy Response* (2018), author and co-editor of *Global Criminal* *and Sovereign Free Economies and the Demise of the Western Democracies: Dark Renaissance* (Routledge, 2015), and is a primary author of the *Small Wars Journal* plutocratic insurgency notes series. She has also published a number of referred and professional works—individually and co-authored—in *Small Wars & Insurgencies, Small Wars Journal, FBI Library Subject Guides*, and in various edited book projects including *Narcos Over the Border* (Routledge, 2011) and *Criminal-States and Criminal-Soldiers* (Routledge, 2008).

ROBERT J. BUNKER is an international security and counterterrorism professional and is presently an adjunct research professor at the Strategic Studies Institute (SSI) of the U.S. Army War College (USAWC) and an instructor with the Safe Communities Institute, University of Southern California. Past associations include Futurist in Residence, Behavioral Research and Instruction Unit at the Federal Bureau of Investigation (FBI) Academy in Quantico, VA and Distinguished Visiting Professor and Minerva Chair at SSI, USAWC. Dr. Bunker holds university degrees in political science, government, social science, anthropology-geography, behavioral science, and history and has undertaken hundreds of hours of specialized counterterrorism and counternarcotics training. He has delivered numerous presentations—including U.S. Congressional Testimony—and has hundreds of publications including numerous books, booklets, reports, papers, articles, response guidance, and research notes. He has published a number of works related to plutocratic and criminal insurgency concerns including editing the *SWJ Plutocratic Insurgency Reader* (2019), authoring and co-editing the book *Global Criminal and Sovereign Free Economies and the Demise of the Western Democracies: Dark Renaissance*

(Routledge, 2015), editing the book *Criminal Insurgencies in Mexico and the Americas* (Routledge, 2012), and authoring the paper *Old and New Insurgency Forms* (SSI USAWC, 2016), as well as being a primary author of the plutocratic insurgency notes series published at *Small Wars Journal*.

Foreword

Rising levels of inequality, both internationally and domestically, represent a societal as well as, increasingly, a national security concern. A strong and robust middle class has long been considered an integral part of American society, required for both the functioning of its industrialized economy and armor and mechanized-infantry based armies as well as the stability of its liberal-democratic governmental system. Such a reality now seems imperiled with the U.S. middle class appearing to be shrinking before our eyes. The authors of this manuscript—one of whom was a former Minerva Chair at the Strategic Studies Institute involved in a broad 'Dark Globalization' research project while with the U.S. Army War College—have been writing and publishing on this topical area of concern for some time now. They approach this important issue from the perspective of what is known as Fourth Epoch theory, that posits that a global transition from the Modern to Post-Modern era is underway which will result in significant changes to both the international system and its dominant Westphalian state-form—as well as the socio-economic classes that exist within it.

The work is divided into sections initially focusing on a general introduction to this topical area including operationalizations of various terms and concepts related to it, an overview of global inequality, an overview of inequality in the United States, and a discussion focusing on the domestic winners and losers stemming from advances in technology and the illicit and sovereign free components of globalized capitalism. The latter has become a form of capitalism that is at odds with the older form of state-moderated capitalism which was more conducive to liberal-democratic state values, institutions, and structures. The work goes on to detail theoretical research—specifically, Fourth Epoch theory and the commercial insurgency construct—that allows us to more broadly contextualize and interpret the data points related to growing levels of inequality and their impact on the U.S socio-economic class structure, focusing on the middle-class. Special attention is then paid to the criminal, plutocratic, and emergent authoritarian insurgency forms (as a component of the commercial construct) with this in mind. Finally, it goes on to address the impact and policy response recommendations for the U.S. government and armed forces as they relate to the various commercial insurgency sub-forms, war over social and political organization, and developing state and environmental integrity themes.

This manuscript will be of significant interest not only to senior U.S. governmental and Department of Defense (DOD) policymakers and planners but also to international and national security professionals as well as those scholars engaging in class structure, globalized capitalism, and plutocracy focused studies in the social and behavioral sciences. In closing, it is our privilege to publish this important work as a *Small Wars Journal* pocket book and hope it will facilitate both reflection and debate on an integral topic related to our nation's socio-economic integrity and liberal-democratic foundations.

Dave Dilegge
Editor-in-Chief
Small Wars Journal

The Strategic Studies Institute of the U.S. Army War College External Research Associates Program financially supported the research and writing of this work. The views expressed in this book are those of the author(s) and do not necessarily reflect the official policy or position of the Department of the Army, the Department of Defense, the Federal Bureau of Investigation, the Department of Justice, or the U.S. Government, or any other U.S. armed service, intelligence or law enforcement agency, or local or state government.

I

Introduction

It is treated as something of a truism that the world is facing a crisis of economic inequality and that this crisis will present social, political, and security challenges to states across the globe.[1] This research monograph first deconstructs this statement and its premise by looking at what is inherently meant by 'economic inequality' and the ways in which this inequality is seen as having an impact either upon various strata of individuals at large or specific strata of individuals as citizens of Western democratic states. It subsequently examines the foreseen implications that inequality—based upon a variety of measures—presents to the social and political makeup of the United States and, moreover, those security challenges it may create specifically for the U.S. military. As an outcome of this analysis, the "winners" and "losers" between nations and within our own broader society are elucidated such that the implications for the ability to maintain a broad-based democratic society are made clear. The work then ties these concerns with broader theoretical literature vis-à-vis recognizable trends in both modern capitalism itself and the greater historical context in which it is found. Finally, it offers a perspective on realistic policy options that can assist the U.S. government and its defense strategies in adapting to these trends in such a way that is beneficial to protecting U.S. values and interests and the quality of life of its citizens in both the national and global contexts. The remainder of this introduction seeks to set the stage by introducing those measures commonly used in assessing inequality, looking at what is actually being measured and suggesting why a broader view must be used when utilizing them in assessment.

Measures of 'Economic Inequality'

Meaningful evaluation of the notion of 'inequality' is impossible without concrete operationalization of what is meant by the term and then often proves difficult. For some, 'inequality' is a broad social indicator, with roots in conceptualizations of disparate means and opportunity, often stemming from inherent class, ethnic, or gender bias. For others, it is specifically an economic measure based upon particular numerical values but, even there, what is measured may be income, wealth, taxation ratios, and/or debt loads—with or without considerations of mitigating factors—and these themselves may be considered alternately on either an individual or aggregate family or household basis. When taken at the national level in a global comparison of states, the term's meaning becomes even more opaque as the degree of inequality between states masks the extent of inequality within them and the true nature of the lived reality of its citizens. Care must be taken not to conflate the results of a single measure of 'economic inequality' with the whole picture. There too must be a recognition that, to a great extent, the meaningfulness of 'inequality' rests on its actual perception in relative terms on the part of citizens themselves, from the global and national on down to the neighborhood level of experience.

The broader sections of this work looking at global (between-state) and U.S./Western (within-state) inequality will address the data regarding these measures in turn. As way of introduction, however, it is illuminating to examine what is meant to be measured by the various types of social and economic indicators and how that affects the outcome of analysis.

Economic Indicators

The meaning of specific 'economic' indicators, in particular, may not be easily ascertained by those outside the field of economic study. It is perhaps best to start with the meaning of the seeming 'gold standard' of measures of economic inequality, the Gini coefficient. Without going into specifics of the equation involved, this coefficient is in actuality a ratio in which 0 (or 0%) equates with a condition of perfect equality whereas 1 (or 100%) equates with a condition of perfect inequality.[2] That is to say, in the former all income is equally distributed and, in the latter, only one individual earns everything. It is most commonly used to evaluate income although it has been applied to the distribution of wealth as well. Esteemed economist in the field of inequality, Anthony Atkinson, describes the measure, with caveats, thus:

> Inequality is measured by the Gini coefficient, which is a single-number summary index of inequality ranging from 0 to 100 per cent, popularized by the Italian statistician Corrado Gini. Implicit in such an index are distributional weights...but these may not be

> evident to the countless researchers who use the Gini coefficient…[W]e need to remember that the index converts a whole distribution to a single number and that there are many different ways in which such a conversion can be made.[3]

Atkinson chose to use this measure—with his own variant—as it had been (and remains) widely used by others. On the other hand, Thomas Piketty, himself a noted economist in the field of inequality, argues that, while the Gini coefficient may be a good snapshot of overall inequality of distribution between groups, the other most common measure of examining distributions of income or wealth by particular decile—such as a comparison, say, of the 90th with the 10th—is "by far the simplest and most intuitive" for looking at within-group inequality as well as "being available in reliable numbers for many countries."[4] A variation of the decile method breaks the unit being considered into quintiles: lower-, lower-middle, middle, upper-middle, and upper income groupings or 'classes.' Income, it should be noted, may refer to simply market income from employment (paycheck or business receipts) or may also include capital income (due to profits from appreciation of an asset which has been sold). Wealth, here, means the economic net worth of an individual (or household) in terms of assets minus debts. As can be seen, one must be extremely cognizant of which methodology is used (e.g. Gini, decile comparisons, or an alternative), which criteria is used (e.g. income—either market or capital—vs. wealth), and what unit of assessment is used (e.g. at the societal level or individual vs. related or unrelated members of a 'household') before any meaningful sense of what is being compared can be made.

Societal Indicators

Whereas the previous indicators can be seen to rest on inputs to an individual or household, other economic indicators also cited in combination and independently as markers of inequality find their basis in outputs or the costs to maintain a certain standard of living within society. These may be based on the price of varying 'baskets of essential goods.' Often, this relates to food or nutrition but also may consider the costs of other aspects of daily life such as housing, transportation, education, and health and child care, for example. Such considerations have formed the basis for the creation within economic study of 'poverty lines' meant to indicate the levels at which income no longer meets these needs. Income as described above may here include tax credits and social transfers meant to ameliorate inequality in access to such necessities, particularly for those at the poverty line. This often is quite different for those in countries at opposite ends of the global inequality spectrum. Alternately, these shortfalls may be expressed in public and family debt levels. Globally, the World Bank measure of poverty rests on those individuals living on somewhere between $1 (extremely poor) and $2 (poor) in USD/day. Clearly, the standard level of poverty in many countries is numerically much higher. The problem here is that, even in the West, some countries—such as the U.S.—use an absolute measure of 'poverty' whereas for others—the EU, for example—it is more relative in nature and involves considerations of social exclusion.[5] This dovetails with other societal indicators of inequality such as inequality of opportunity (e.g. access to education, health care, and the political process) and relative means for social mobility. The importance of the latter goes hand-in-glove with the existence of a thriving segment of the population existing within the middle levels of society.

The Middle Class

A significant and increasingly used societal indicator when considering inequality is thus that of the size and economic health of what may be termed the 'middle class.' While the 90/10 decile comparison mentioned above is common, it compares income percentages between the top and bottom deciles. The middle class—by definition somewhere in the middle of the distribution—is contrastingly often considered in terms of the middle three of five 'quintiles' of the population. The span of income alone between these quintiles, however, can vary by over $100,000 USD.[6] In terms of measurement of its health or growth, as with those experiencing 'poverty,' it may be singled out by relative or absolute levels of income or other indicators—there is no single official definition of what constitutes the 'middle class.' Pew Research, for example, considers "middle-income" Americans to be those adults whose annual household income is two-thirds to double the national median, after incomes have been adjusted for household size.[7] A Brookings Institution report, on the other hand, finds the American middle class can be described alternately by its "cash, credentials, and culture" (basically, its income and wealth, education and career track, and lifestyle and aspirations), although they too note economists most commonly base it on some form of median income.[8] Furthermore, any measures must be adjusted for regional (and indeed micro-regional) cost of living. Consequently, one can imagine the difficulty of coming up with any meaningful statistical measure meant to define a homogenous 'global middle class.' One such attempt at creating a globally comparative measure in 2000 set the bar for being 'middle class' at between $12 and $50 USD per person per day but, more generally, for developing countries, the 'middle class' has been said to be those living on between $2 and $10.[9] Using a

$10 to $50 benchmark, a 2011 Pew study found "almost nine-in-ten Americans had a standard of living that was above the global middle-income standard."[10] Often, however, those deemed in the "middle" have incomes—not to mention wealth—far below the midpoint of the extremes in income found within a society and their definition as "middle" appears almost by default of being neither super-rich nor existing at or below the poverty line. Still, Mario Pezzini of the Organization for Economic Cooperation and Development (OECD) has highlighted the current changing nature of the middle class in the developed and developing world—with the former shrinking as the latter grows. Beyond these changes, he finds the vulnerability of both sets of middle classes troubling since:

> …middle classes are not only a motor of consumption and domestic demand, their social role remains equally important. Middle classes are believed to support democracy and progressive but moderate political platforms. Strong middle classes can influence economic development through active participation in the political process, expressing support for political programmes and electoral platforms, in particular those that promote inclusive growth.[11]

This study will argue that, after examining the data regarding the range of the economic and societal indicators outlined above, reversing the trend towards the polarization resulting from the declining size and role of a true middle class within our American and indeed other Western societies is at the forefront in mitigating the most significant challenges to our core values and security in the face of the epochal change before us.

II

Global Inequality

Global (in terms of overall between-state) inequality has long been of interest in the United States for both humanitarian and practical considerations as the gap in income and wealth between 'developed' and 'developing' (sometimes historically termed core-periphery or first and third world states) meant that many countries found themselves in need of some form of economic assistance either directly from other national governments, such as the U.S., or through the intervention of large international organizations. Further, economic inequality is a primary factor driving migration between regions, for example the continued influx of migrants from Mexico seeking work in the United States, particularly to its border states, although their numbers have been dropping for a variety of reasons.[12] Moreover, due to a number of factors, those countries suffering at the low end of the income inequality spectrum have also been more subject to more political instability, crime, and corruption—negatively impacting both their own populations as well as having spillover effects to the world at large.[13] Political vacuums often form, allowing for the spread of criminality such as trade in illicit goods, human trafficking, and terrorism. Such instability and criminal activity also drives legal and illegal migration to the United States, largely from countries in Latin—particularly Central—America and Asia as their citizens seek safe refuge. Perceptions of threats posed by such groups can also have repercussions for the U.S. military. The White house has recently ordered 5,200 active duty troops to the U.S.-Mexico border in anticipation of the arrival of two caravans of migrants from Central America seeking asylum in the U.S. The same number of troops are currently in Iraq to keep watch against the Islamic State.[14] Given all of these factors, the potential impact on global inequality has also become an important consideration of research seeking to evaluate the effects of the ongoing acceleration in the globalization and technologizing of trade.

Global measures of economic inequality—based in large part on individual countries' own national household surveys—often attempt to express information on global income in a way that reflects purchasing power parity (PPP) by using data from the International Comparison Project (ICP) which measures prices in each country for roughly equivalent baskets of goods.[15] The good news would seem to be that—based on measures of the Gini coefficient—the relative national income gap is closing for many nations.[16] According to the World Bank Group, in light of the continued rise in global inequality since the early 19th century, there was an unprecedented drop in global inequality as manifested in the between-nations Gini index (with adjustment for purchasing power parity) beginning in 1988, when it was .668, through 2013, when it was .625. The authors also note that this decline occurred during a period of increasing global integration.[17] Researchers with the United Nations University World Institute for Development

(UNU-WIDER) determined, with slightly different numbers, a similar trend in the decline of between-nation income inequality but beginning earlier with a Gini value of 0.739 in 1975 falling to one of 0.631 in 2010. Those authors, however, contrasted this decline in relative inequality with a concurrent dramatic increase in absolute income inequality—based on differentials between absolute monetary totals of income rather than percent changes—which they deem significant.[18] These same authors have maintained elsewhere that there is a factor of "global interpersonal inequality" that is not accounted for in the typical between-country measures of global inequality but which is "inherent in the actual global distribution of income, of all citizens of the world." While its measurement is more complex, what it does is take into account actual distributions of income rather than "what the inequality among all the individuals in the world would be if each person received the average per capita income for his/her country."[19]

There is of course an argument to be made that a certain amount of absolute inequality is necessary for economic "progress,"[20] but the numbers paint a far different picture vis-à-vis the true state of global inequality—one in which the very rich only get exponentially richer compared to the rest of society—as will be seen in what follows. While much has been written about the effects of globalization in terms of the implications of the widespread mobilization of capital, pertinent here is the emphasis found in William Robinson's work that what is being experienced today is "a relatively new epoch in the ongoing evolution of world capitalism" which is truly "transnational" in nature even as the nation-state "does not disappear or even become 'less important.'"[21] He finds the contradiction of "a globalizing economy within a nation-state based political system," however, has led to an inability to adequately address economic crises. As global society reconfigures around a globalized economy, inequality thus is beginning to crystallize differently—with society "increasingly stratified less along national and territorial lines than across social and class lines."[22] While we may be seeing convergence in Gini coefficients at a global 'between-state' level, income and wealth are overarchingly becoming increasingly more polarized between the 'have' and 'have-nots.' Inequality *within* states has become a global disorder.

Christopher Lakner and Branco Milanovic sought to express these shifts in graphic form through what would become known colloquially as the 'elephant chart.'[23] When the points between deciles are joined, the graph of relative gains in real per capita income between 1988-2008 appears to show the rough outline of an elephant with four main points of interest. To its far left, are those countries—mostly African nations—who have made slight gains but remain at the bottom of the global income distribution. At its center—the highest point or 'back' of the elephant—Milanovic finds the poor and middle class populations of the emerging Asian economies, which then can be contrasted with a group to its right—at a higher global income yet which has appeared to stagnate—believed to represent the middle and lower middle classes in OECD countries. Finally, further to the right still, at the highest point of the elephant's 'trunk' can be found what he refers to as the 'global plutocrats,' those individuals comprising the world's wealthiest (predominantly American) 1 percent.[24] As with the World Bank study mentioned above, Milanovic notes that things look much different when considered in absolute rather than relative terms. In this case, the rising Asian lower and middle classes and the OECD middle class look more similar in terms of approximately 2 and 3% of gains, respectively, while the top

5% of the wealthiest among the global population received 44% of the absolute gains in income. The lowest income countries, in contrast, have made little absolute gains at all.[25]

This study gained a lot of attention and critiques of Milanovic's presentation and/or interpretation of the elephant chart are well-known.[26] Part of the concern was that the chart covers a period in which there was marked reintegration of both Eastern Europe and China into the world economic system as well as a period in which Japan experienced uncharacteristic stagnation. Additionally, the data stops in 2008, the onset of the 'Great Recession.' By extending the data to 2016, the 2018 World Inequality Report gets a much flatter curve. Yet, despite the reported use of different data sources, the main points of the original graph—the rise of emerging countries, a squeezed 90% at the bottom in the West, and the prosperity of the global 1 percent—once again find expression.[27] Some interesting new findings include: (1) that at the global level, inequality has risen sharply since 1980, despite strong growth in China; (2) that, although there has been a slight decline in the rise of global inequality since 2000, this has been due to a reduction in between-country average income inequality rather than any decrease within-country; and (3) that the global wealth middle class continues to be squeezed—if not exactly stagnant—due to that rising within-country wealth inequality.[28]

Homi Kharas argued in 2017 that there had actually been an expansion of the global middle class such that perhaps by the year 2020 a majority of the world's population would live in middle-class or rich households, with the overwhelming majority of these in Asia. But the largest growth in these, he admits, are on the lower end, coming from the emerging economies and thus may be unsustainable in the long term—as those governments cannot necessarily rely on the levels of taxation needed to provide essential services such as health care and public education nor does the existence of a middle class in these countries ensure the demand for democratic governance.[29] Further, as others have pointed out, Kharas' definition ranges between those whose individual annual income is between $4,000 and $40,000/year based on country of residence—i.e. those who make enough to cover basic needs with "something left over."[30] The argument that individuals will be content with that level of existence discounts the relative nature of deprivation both within and beyond one's immediate community. In a time where few communities are isolated from a knowledge of affluence due to the expansion of globalization (luxury goods are being made by the very poorest) and the pervasiveness of digital technology, it is easy to see how resentment could fester without a true national if not necessarily global 'middle class' fostering a sense of achievable social mobility.

The rise of an economic strata out of range from the rest of the world's population are echoed by the results of many studies which, moreover, have found that, if anything, the results are skewed towards masking the full extent of inequality due to a lack of complete information from the extreme low and extreme high income groups. Oxfam used data from Credit Suisse to conclude in 2018 that "the world's 42 richest people are worth the same as the 3.7 billion who make up the poorest half of the world's population."[31] Reacting to Oxfam's findings, anthropologist Jason Hickel looked at figures from the Maddison Historical Statistics Project at the University of Groningen, Netherlands. He asserts that, due to the balance of power in the global economy, in absolute terms global inequality has continued to increase by orders of magnitude over the past 200 years. From 1960 to today, he finds "the absolute gap between the average incomes of people in the richest and poorest countries has grown by 135%."[32] Oxfam puts the problem this way:

> Between 1990 and 2010, the number of people living in extreme poverty (i.e. on less than $1.90 a day) halved, and has continued to decline since then. This tremendous achievement is something of which the world should be proud. Yet had inequality within countries not grown during that period, an extra 200 million people would have escaped poverty. This number could have risen to 700 million had poor people benefited more from economic growth than their rich fellow citizens.[33]

Recent studies, drawing upon new data points reflecting the multiple and overlapping challenges of globalization, have come to many of the same conclusions that have driven theoretical constructs of an author of this monograph—many of which were first proposed by that author three decades ago. Those constructs, focusing on societal level epochal change and the energy foundations upon which they are configured will be set out in a later monograph section. Here, suffice it to say that there is a broadening recognition that the new technology of the digital age is transformative in nature, such that the downstream effects will result in significant dislocation in human employment patterns with automation of even non-routine tasks, and unprecedented in speed, such that it is giving global society far less time to adapt to those changes.[34]

The social unease which has arisen from the dual processes of the globalization and technologizing of trade has further politically polarized already economically polarized populations in the developed world. Yet these processes are here to stay and are not directly to blame. A recent *Foreign Affairs* piece, "Globalization Is Not in Retreat," counters the notion that it has somehow been reversed by the downturn of the 2008 financial crisis. Instead, the authors find globalization has merely entered a new phase—no longer trade-based and Western-led but rather "driven by digital technology" and increasingly led by China and other emerging economies. In this new phase, they acknowledge jobs will be lost as certain sectors are no longer relevant but hold the negative effects are self-inflicted:

> Globalization has its winners and losers, and in theory, the gains should be big enough to compensate the losers. But, in practice, the benefits have rarely been distributed, and the communities and workers harmed by globalization have turned to populism and protection.[35]

Zia Qureshi—former director of development economics at the World Bank—would seem to agree. He attributes the common sense of our living in a 'fractured world,' as expressed by the World Economic Forum in Davos, to the fact that while "the world has not become less prosperous," economic growth has slowed and its benefits are becoming increasingly unequally shared. He recognizes that globalization and technology are forces that create "winners and losers" but contends that it is governmental policy that has not ensured that the economic gains are more widely shared.[36] The authors of the *World Inequality Report* similarly find that—since countries at similar levels of development are exhibiting some differences in inequality levels—policies can help shape the outcome at the national level.[37]

Policies of the richer countries with regard to the less developed of the world also can contribute to bettering conditions for all. Economist and policy analyst Jeffrey Sachs writes that the United States cannot be "an island of stability and prosperity in a global sea of poverty and unrest." Beyond humanitarian concerns, the historical record of global economic failures of states which have led to political failures with far-reaching consequences worldwide is too vast, he notes, to ignore the potential costs to U.S. strategic interests in terms of national security (where political vacuums lead to criminality, such as money laundering, trafficking, and terrorism), threats to U.S. businesses and economic stakes abroad, and public health (such as the international spread of pathogens affecting the food supply and global pandemics).[38] But national sovereignty in the form of the political will to make even some of these policy changes—such as increasingly progressive taxes and needed social redistribution along with better access to education and new forms of job training in line with new developments in technology, not to mention policies addressing threatened economic failure abroad—appears to have been co-opted due to influence by those whose allegiance is to extra-national capitalist ends. If indeed it is true that 82% of the global wealth generated in 2017 went to the wealthiest 1%,[39] then the further issue is that the problem of global inequality has become transnational—the ability for a single nation to clamp down on those seeking to remove themselves from taxation and/ or accountability in business practices is becoming impossible without the ability to act at a level that is international in nature and scope. In the next section, the implications of within-state inequality—specifically, within the United States but with some reference to its Western allies—will be discussed in more detail.

III

Inequality Within the United States

In 2015, the United States was found to hold 41.6% of global personal wealth ($63.5 trillion),[40] reflecting the relative global affluence of its citizens. Further, in reviewing the world panel income distribution data used by Lakner and Milanovic in creating the original 'elephant chart,' a Resolution Foundation study noted that, overall, the mature Western economies during the 1988-2008 period performed well in income growth when compared to the rest of the world (omitting China). However, they also found these growth rates were widely dispersed, with the United States one of the worst performers in terms of equality of distribution among its citizens. While on average U.S. income grew by 2% per year, it acknowledged, these gains were markedly "skewed towards the richest."[41] It is not surprising to find then that in 2017, the OECD ranked the United States at .39 on the Gini coefficient index for *net* income inequality (that is, after taxes and transfers), up from 34.6 in 1979. With one of the highest scores of the OECD countries, it was closer to Turkey at .40 than other mature Western democracies such as Germany or France, both at .29. The U.S. had the next to

                    Small Wars Journal

highest Gini ranking among the G7 nations.[42] In 2016, in contrast, the EU-wide Gini coefficient hit an almost three-decade low.[43] The Gini ranking for the United States does vary somewhat by state with Alaska closest to the national average at .4174 while New York showed highest inequality levels with a Gini of .51.[44] Studies conducted by the International Monetary Fund (IMF) have shown that, while some inequality at the level of below .27 on the net Gini scale can be beneficial, those at higher levels can have serious negative economic and societal consequences.[45]

To look at this from another perspective, while the inclusion of taxes and transfers in the equation do significantly increase average household income growth rates for the lower quintiles, the latest U.S. Congressional Budget Office data shows that, despite this, "the top 1 percent of the income distribution experienced the largest cumulative growth in income after transfers and taxes" with real income for that group 228% greater than in 1979.[46] In comparison to Western Europe, in 1980 the 1% in both groups held 10% of total income in their respective regions but, by 2016, the American top 1% had 20% of income while the European group held just 12%.[47] Using data from another source and considering U.S. working age households adjusted for family size, the Resolution Foundation goes even further in concluding that the years 2007-2013 actually saw declining real incomes for all except the top decile.[48] The *World Inequality Report* provides some insight in that in the U.S.:

> Compared to the period between 1940 and 1960 when the level of taxation of the top 1% was consistently above 40%, the average tax rate as a percentage of pre-tax income was more than five percentage points lower in 2014, and

ten percentage points lower than before the financial crisis. In contrast to the overall fall in tax rates for the top earners since the 1940s, taxes on the bottom 50% have risen from 15% to 25% between 1940 and 2014.[49]

These 2014 figures are likely to become even more pronounced as a result of the recently passed December 2017 Tax Cuts and Jobs Act and ongoing efforts to reduce redistributive policies such as Medicare and Social Security. In an independent evaluation, the Tax Policy Center determined that the biggest benefits "relative to current tax burdens, relative to income, and in dollar terms" would accrue to the highest income groups.[50]

The current levels of inequality in United States are magnified when overall wealth is factored in. A National Bureau of Economic Research report finds that wealth inequality in the United States climbed in the 2007-2010 period as the middle class suffered far greater—largely from the drop in housing prices—than did the top percentiles during this same period, who have a more diverse set of investments and rebounded more quickly.[51] In 2015, Allianz Financial Services' *Global Wealth Report* found the U.S. wealth gap greater than that of income, assigning it a Gini coefficient for wealth at a staggering .8056.[52] In 2018, Allianz developed a new measure as an alternative to the wealth Gini coefficient. Its 2018 Allianz Wealth Equity Indicator (AWEI) ranks countries from 1 (very good) to 7 (poor) in terms of wealth distribution based on five different indicators. It ranked the U.S. as a seven. Moreover, it found that while the U.S. ranked second in terms of average financial assets per capita in 2017, it fell to fourteenth when median assets were considered—falling out of the top ten completely.[53]

Wealth inequality, of course, is not just a U.S. problem. A study commissioned by the UK House of Commons determined that the global 1% will control 64 percent—nearly two-thirds—of all global wealth by the year 2030.[54] Furthermore, while 'national' wealth in the form of private wealth has boomed, the public wealth of the U.S.—like many nominally 'rich' countries—has gone negative due to its heavy debt load, tax cuts for the top brackets, and continued deficit spending.[55] But as with income inequality above, the problem in the United States comes into sharper focus when it is compared with other mature Western democracies. The *World Inequality Report*—with the caveat that the available data is much sparser than for income—finds that in the U.S. wealth inequality for the 0.1% has snowballed over the last 30 years due to the growing overall inequality of income and savings rates whereas the increase in France and the UK was more moderate due to its lower income inequality and rising housing wealth for the middle classes in those countries.[56]

Overall, the top 10% of American families are thought to own 75% of U.S. household wealth and the top 0.1% as much as the bottom 90%.[57] Dow Jones' *MarketWatch* reports that "America's 1% hasn't controlled this much wealth since before the Great Depression," noting that while Amazon's Jeff Bezos has a net worth surpassing $150 billion, the median net worth of Americans as a whole is $68,828 per household.[58] Half of households fall above and below this figure and this figure includes home equity. Jim Wang of *Business Insider* explains that equity is 75.39% of total net worth therefore, in actuality, the median net worth excluding equity for all Americans falls more accurately at $16,942.[59] The ramifications become clearer when actual household savings is considered. A Federal Reserve Report on the Economic Well-Being of U.S. Households in 2017 surveying more than 12,000 households reports that while 74% of adults reported they were financially okay or 'comfortable,' 4 in 10 still said they could not meet an emergency expense of $400 without using credit, borrowing, or selling something. Furthermore, according to the report, over one-fifth of adults are unable to pay each month's bills in full and less than two-fifths of nonretired adults think their retirement savings are on track.[60]

In the world's wealthiest country, many Americans find themselves living on an economic knife's edge. In this, the United States finds company in some in the developed world, albeit to a slightly lesser degree. In the UK, for example, due to part-time, no benefits employment and the high cost of food and housing, 41% of those surveyed had under £1,000 ($1,285) in savings and 32 percent had less than £500 ($642). Similarly, 40 percent did not expect to save enough for a decent standard of living in retirement.[61] The U.S. findings may seem counter-intuitive given the generally positive outlook on the American economy presented by economists. The OECD economic forecast for the U.S., for example, shows economic growth at around 3% and only 3.7% unemployment.[62] According to the U.S. Census, the real median household income for 2017 was $61,372, the highest it has ever been, although it has cautioned that its methodology has changed and may not be directly comparable to previous years.[63] But, by definition, it should be remembered once again that half of U.S. households make less than this and many remain employed in part-time and low wage positions. The number of Americans in poverty in 2017 was 39.7 million, by the U.S. Census' calculation "not statistically different" from 2016.[64] According to the U.S. Department of Housing and Urban Development, a biennial street count in 2017 determined there were approximately 554,000 homeless on any given night—up for the first time in seven years and likely undercounted.[65]

While comparison of the top and bottom within American society offers a striking contrast, perhaps the biggest indicator of the long-term economic and social health of the nation is to be found in the strength of its middle class for all the reasons mentioned in the introductory remarks above. A middle class drives economic consumption and demand, serves as a stabilizing and moderating force for the political process, and provides a platform for social mobility which can ease social tensions. Or at least it did. It was noted above that the interaction between the 'middle class' and the government in emerging economies may not have that same relationship but it is precisely those middle class populations which are booming. In the United States, however, the sense is one of a class that is slowly disappearing, or perhaps more accurately, one which is becoming meaningless due to both the enormous gap between it and the national and global elite and internal divisions. Some consider the U.S. as "no longer one country" but closer to a developing nation, divided in half by "resources, expectations, and fates."[66]

While this may be more prognostication than current reality, nonetheless several indicators do point in this direction for the future. Some ways to look at the health of the middle class include income, wealth, consumption, education, and health. It was noted earlier the difficulties in actually pinpointing who qualifies as 'middle class' in terms of income brackets— e.g. middle quintiles, relation to the poverty line, or median income—as well as the complicating factors of availability, accuracy, and timeliness of data. Robert Reich points out that while the unemployment rate is remarkably low, work is often contract or part-time with no benefits or security, wages actually dropped in the second quarter of the year, and many college educated workers are overqualified for their jobs. He finds a declining share of total U.S. income going to the middle quintiles stemming back to the 1960s and correlating directly with a decline in unionization and bargaining power.[67] Over the last ten years, the median income of the top quintile is said to have increased at 1.5 times the growth rate of the middle fifth, based on U.S. Census data.[68] This can be contrasted with the UK where middle brackets saw slightly faster income growth than those at the top and bottom deciles, due in part to increased employment and the institution of a National Living Wage.[69] Some cite predatory fees on the debt that Americans increasingly rely on to maintain a middle-class lifestyle—particularly due to the exorbitant costs of housing and education—with draining the wealth of that middle strata.[70] *Financial Times* describes the life of this "Middle Precariat" as one in which educated professionals work well over 40 hours a week in order to stay ahead of an economy with stagnant wages and inadequate safety nets and maintain a middle class life while paying for increasingly expensive housing, education, healthcare, and childcare.[71]

It is generally agreed that consumption levels—like income and wealth—are also problematic ways to determine middle class status, here due to the problems of measurement errors, weighting purchases with debt and savings, and transfers and in-kind transactions. Nonetheless, researchers have questioned whether consumption of goods and leisure might reveal different insights than income with regard to rich, middle, and poor households and/or provide a better measure of changes in welfare. Orazio Attanasio and Luigi Pistaferri, from University College London and Stanford University, respectively, found that while there needs to be a better way to adjust for quality changes "there is little evidence of growing inequality in caloric intakes," but nonetheless "inequality in the consumption of nondurables and services has increased substantially over the past few decades," paralleling income inequality.[72] The Washington Center for Equitable Growth adds that the different strata have been shown in several recent studies to have different consumption baskets creating differential inflation rates which favor those at the top.[73] Unfortunately, the pathways to mobility in today's society are also lined with the kinds of economic choices that are putting it out of the reach of many. In a country where there is still a belief in the Horatio Alger stories of success based on merit alone, the hard fact is that growing up in elite communities, going to elite colleges, and socializing in elite circles are the more likely routes to who you marry, your future job prospects, and your ultimate ranking in society. The top percent may succeed due to hard work and innovation but, as Chrystia Freeland points out, most did not start out at the bottom and they have more in common with a transglobal community of peers than their fellow citizens at home.[74]

In a noted speech from January 2012, Alan B. Krueger, Chairman of the Council of Economic Advisers, drawing attention to the decline in the American middle class, observes:

> ...the persistence in the advantages and disadvantages of income passed from parents to the children is predicted to rise by about a quarter for the next generation as a result of the rise in inequality that the U.S. has seen in the last 25 years. It is hard to look at these figures and not be concerned that rising inequality is jeopardizing our tradition of equality of opportunity. The fortunes of one's parents seem to matter increasingly in American society.[75]

Kreuger is not just noting the passing on of large sums of inherited wealth between the generations, although that is also a factor. More to the point, he is recognizing with concern that the advantages provided by being born to a well-off generation sets the next generation up circumstantially for further social mobility which they then pass on to their children. These advantages end up reflected in statistics for marriage rates, education, and housing. A study by Pew Research Center finds that, while marriage rates in America are dropping, those who do get married make the highest incomes. They, in turn, link these developments to college education levels.[76] Following Kreuger's line of thinking above, those who go to elite colleges are likely to meet potential spouses who also come from similar backgrounds with similar advantages—if not, they can meet them in their upper class neighborhoods—and so the cycle continues. College in the United States is more expensive than anywhere else in the world. Journalist Rana Faroohar finds that, during the Eisenhower administration, governmental funding for college was considered to the benefit of national security whereas now, with funding cuts, Americans typically accrue $30,000 in student debt.[77] An article by Amanda Ripley explores this issue further. She notes that, as a result of these cuts, colleges started acting more like businesses and, as with health care, being market driven can make these systems innovative but also exploitative as there is no price capping mechanisms as in other developed countries, like the UK.[78] The follow-on is that this favors the wealthy as student debt and its servicing can follow individuals (and/or their parents) prohibiting funding of their future retirement.[79]

In these ways, where one starts also impacts where they and their children ultimately live which in turn fuels the cycle again. A Brookings Report finds that "there is a great divergence in the prosperity of whole communities and regions of the country" and even "the destinies and futures of middle-class households varies sharply by geography."[80] As the middle class shrinks, there has been a concurrent growth in communities segregated by income levels within larger metropolitan areas. While the share of families living in middle class neighborhoods was reported to have dropped from 65 to 40% between 1970 and 2012, those living in all-poor or all-affluent ones were said to have doubled.[81] Where the middle class has survived, the change in the gap between upper-rich and middle class has been noted to have widened in 98 of 100 metropolitan areas.[82] A couple of examples are illustrative. An example at the high end can be found in California's 'Silicon Valley,' driven by the expansion of the highly paid tech industry. One study compared the average incomes for households in the top and bottom quintiles. San Jose showed an expansion in the 'rich versus poor gap' of $73,600, pushing that difference in incomes between these groups to $339,000. In examining the 'middle class span' between the middle quintiles (specifically, between the 30% versus 80% groups), the gap grew the most in nearby San Francisco where it rose $32,500 to a $140,800 difference in average incomes between these groups.[83] According to the Department of Housing and Urban Development, the median price of a single family home in the wider San Francisco Bay area has risen to $935,000, but mere shells of homes in San Francisco proper are selling for over $1 million—a 64% rise over the last 5 years. Accordingly, a household income of $117,000 is now considered "low income" for that region.[84] The bar to entry has been raised even for many of those born and raised nearby, forcing them into long commutes or out of the Bay area completely. The converse of this can be seen in Stilwell, Oklahoma, in the foothills of the Ozarks. Andrew Van Dam reports that Stilwell is in the bottom 25% nationwide for income with a low average level of education and a high crime rate. Moreover, it suffers the lowest life expectancy in the nation at 56.3 years—22.5 years below the nation average.[85] In 2016, the median income in Stilwell of the 1,381 total households was $24,135, a decline from the previous year, and the median property value was $73,600, although most rent rather than own.[86] However, people living in several wealthier nearby communities reportedly have a life expectancy into their 90s, reflecting the uneven opportunity for health and well-being presented by the segregational aspects of inequality.[87] Those born and raised in Stilwell, however, face an uphill battle to leave.

Ultimately, the importance of what has just been considered goes back to the definition of the 'middle class' in terms of its aspirations and what it represents for the nation as a whole. A 2010 Middle Class Task Force sought to concretely list what constituted those aspirations. In short, it was the economic stability to own a home, have a comfortable retirement, education and healthcare for themselves and their children, cars for the adults and family vacations each year. Reviewing this list, a Brooking Report concedes that it is not in desiring these things that determines one's economic class but the ease of achieving them.[88] To extrapolate, it might be said, the lower classes feel they can't achieve them, the middle classes must work hard to possibly achieve them, and the upper echelons take these achievements as a given. Herein lies the source of social frustrations. To hear of tax cuts for elite individuals and corporations—or worse, endless deferments and outright evasion—while their own family is struggling amounts to cheating in the eyes of this middle group, which values hard work and merit. The idea of an "unashamedly predatory" strata which sucks the nation dry while failing to reinvest its disproportionate wealth in either through providing employment or paying full taxation thereby funding societal welfare programs has led Paul Kennedy to coin the term "vampire capitalism."[89] Combine this with the fact that it has been recognized that many U.S. elites enjoy "strategic citizenship" wherein, through dual citizenship, these mobile individuals and families enjoy the privileges of citizenship in multiple countries while avoiding the "traditional duties associated with formal membership." Social anthropologists Yossi Harpaz and Pablo Mateos refer to this as a "de-sacralization" of citizenship which challenges the "equality" and "shared fate" associated with the idea of a national citizenry.[90] Chrystia Freeland finds America's elites are adjusting to this global perspective. She quotes a senior executive as arguing that the hollowing out of the middle class really didn't matter and should take a pay cut since he "could get workers anywhere in the world."[91] Citizenship further seems to be up for sale. Peter Thiel, the American billionaire co-founder of Paypal, reportedly was granted New Zealand citizenship having spent no more than 12 days in the country. To add another layer, seven Silicon Valley entrepreneurs are said to have purchased underground 'survival bunkers' in New Zealand in 2018 as a hedge against anything from public uprisings to bioterrorism, seeking to privatize their own security.[92]

If citizenship is being bartered to see which country offers the best deal, it is of little wonder that those unable to engage in the new strategic globalism have turned to nationalism in its wake. Solt presents evidence that "across the advanced democracies and over time, where [domestic] economic inequality is greater, nationalist sentiments are substantially more widespread." The problem is, he finds, that this 'nationalism' often fosters threat inflation that both turns hostility inward towards immigrants and minorities and outward inflating dangers from abroad[93]

This can be seen in certain polarizing rhetoric seen in the U.S. today and there are concerns that it may affect the U.S. military in a number of ways. In one direct example, Hazel Atuel, professor of Social Work at USC, has begun studying social identity and the military in response to a U.S. Department of Homeland Security concern about extreme ideologies among service members and recruitment of veterans. While potential radicalism by Islamic extremists has been the dominant narrative, given recent acts of right-wing terrorism in the U.S. "fueled by an increasingly volatile political climate," nationalist extremist ideologies among those in military service have become a pressing concern.[94] In 2017, quite controversially, there were accusations of nationalist extremism in the ranks and in May 2018 there was a congressional call for an investigation into these allegations.[95] In the past, service in the U.S. military was seen as an "equalizer" within U.S. society. An op-ed by former Marine, Benjamin Luxembourg makes the point that the military has been America's "last bastion of social and economic equality" in which salaries are closer between the ranks, they intermingle on bases and their children go to the same schools, and hardships forge trust and bonds between those from different backgrounds. However, as he laments, among elected officials in 2015 prior military service was at 20 percent—an all-time low—and fewer than 1% of Ivy League graduates chose to serve. He finds the growing civil-military gap is increased by and further increases social stratification.[96] The change in both the size of the military services and their mission profiles, however, has been found to also be changing their makeup and thus their role as employers, educators, and means of upward mobility. A 2013 study by Andrea Asoni and Tino Sanandaji looked at representativeness in the modern military and determined that the turn towards a smaller and more technologically advanced military has made it more selective in recruitment, shifting demographics away from minorities due to less access to quality secondary education and with both the very poor and the rich under-represented.[97]

A cross-national study on the military and income inequality has found that the new "capital-intensive" military—with sizable investments in high-tech weaponry combined with a reduction in military jobs—ultimately exacerbates economic inequality. The reduction in casualties by this same equipment (pilotless drones, smart bombs, and the like) makes military conflicts much more palatable.[98] With nationalist sentiment seen as inflating threats combined with the decreasing number of elites and policymakers serving in the military, the potential to involve the armed forces more readily—and potentially inadvisably— in conflicts is a distinct possibility. Concurrently, the desire for reductions in overall governmental expenditures while the technology of modern peacekeeping and warfare is becoming more expensive further fuels broader public perceptions that there is a tradeoff between such spending and a reduction in social programs such as health and education. Increasingly too, active duty troops are being called on to participate in "gray area" operations, such as their employment at the U.S.-Mexico border, where they face legal limits to their activities due to "posse comitatus." Although there are no official figures as yet, the cost of those operations have been estimated at up to $10 million per day.[99] The public is sensitive to the costs of troop deployment. An article by former U.S. Army intelligence officer Chris Davis points out that the cost of the Global War on Terrorism was in the trillions of dollars without the sense of a correlating increase in American security, exacerbating the economic crisis which was felt sharply by the middle class which bears the heaviest burden of financing wars and their consequences. All the while, he notes "[i]ncreasingly expensive and complex weapon systems reduce the availability of military forces, and restrict their flexibility by requiring them to operate equipment and execute doctrines ill-suited for the demands of war."[100] What the public sees are cuts in taxes for those at the top on one hand and increased military expenditures with a reduction in military jobs on the other—a lose-lose proposition for most.

George Sayers Bain writes that, if as has been suggested markets have moral limits, then "inequality has social and political as well as economic consequences" in which persistent inequality erodes the trust of the people in its government, undermining the cohesion of democratic societies.[101] The UN Secretary General addressed the General Assembly in September 2018 with the words of caution that "inequality is undermining faith in the social contract."[102] Cross-nationally, there are strong indications that inequality—particularly at ties of overall economic growth—is a strong driver of support for violent extremism[103] and the greater the disparity in wealth, the greater the risk of internal uprisings and even civil war.[104] Domestically, at best, it creates incentives for criminal behavior and results in higher property crime in richer neighborhoods.[105] At worst, it creates escalating polarization that results in the type of unreasonable behavior that becomes ungovernable.[106] The next section looks at the winners and losers resulting from the inequality found today in the United States and the resulting ramifications of those divisions.

IV

The Winners and the Losers

As can be expected, the increasing rise in inequality in the United States—and the collinear loss of the middle class structure which serves as a dampening force on extreme polarization of poverty and wealth in our country—is resulting in the emergence of new winners and new losers domestically. Modern state-moderated capitalism has long been viewed as promoting a win-win outcome where everyone within a liberal-democratic society—especially the children of new immigrants—benefit, with high social mobility potentials existing for the lower classes (especially if they worked hard and diligently). Such perceptions were enshrined in 1883 by the American poet Emma Lazarus who penned a sonnet— about the Statue of Liberty that would be dedicated in New York harbor a few years later and eventually inscribed in a bronze plaque placed upon it—in these six lines:

> "Keep, ancient lands, your storied pomp!" cries she
> With silent lips. "Give me your tired, your poor,
> Your huddled masses yearning to breathe free,

The wretched refuse of your teeming shore.
Send these, the homeless, tempest-tost to me,
I lift my lamp beside the golden door!"[107]

Such perceptions have since shifted—based on the increasing lack of mobility in American society supported by both present Gini coefficients and decile comparisons of income and wealth—due to the rise of predatory, criminalized, and sovereign-free forms of globalized capitalism that have emerged. Even our acceptance of the 'huddled masses' has changed to increasing exclusionary policies as a result of echoes from the collective psychic shock of the 9-11 attacks and unrestrained migration fears on our Southern border due to hemispheric— even global—state fragility and failure.

Where capitalism was once considered a win-win economic system in the West, it has now shifted (or quite possibly reverted) to a more mercantilist competition, resulting in win-lose outcomes representative of the early modern and absolutist eras in the West (and indicative of more proto-capitalism and predatory economic ideologies).[108] It results in a small number of big winners and many losers (See Table 1.). While such win-lose outcomes were long associated with the 'developed' and 'less developed' world (also known historically as core and periphery or first and third world) interactions, the fact that these transactions have since shifted to individual economic interchanges between citizenry in the U.S.—and the rest of the West—with big business and multinational corporations celebrated for their high extractive capacity skills and resulting stock dividends, has become a game changer. These moneymaking machines of the elite classes have gotten so good at generating wealth that schemes such as Payday Advance (in which future worker paychecks are sold at a discount), dynamic online pricing using AI algorithms, and even agreements in which a % of future professional incomes are mortgaged against college education costs—resembling a 21st century form of indentured-servitude to transnational investment funds—are being implemented.[109] These schemes represent only the tip of the iceberg of an extractive process aimed at the middle and lower classes whom—should they become buried in personal debt—will find it increasingly difficult to discharge, particularly since that debt may have actually even been purchased on the secondary investment market.[110]

CATEGORIES	THE WINNERS	THE LOSERS
SOCIAL CLASSES	- The Upper (Highly Skilled, Creative, Wealthy, Connected)	- The Lower & Middle (Un- & Semi-Skilled; Blue-Collar; Middle Management)
BUSINESSES	- Multinational Corporations - Informational-Internet Technology Based	- Local-to-National Companies - Industrial Technology and Brick & Mortar Based
ECONOMIES	-Sovereign-Free & Illicit	-Formal
POLITICAL PARTIES	- Polarizing Elites & Fringe Factions	- Democratic and Republican Moderates - Independents (Opt Outs)
GOVERNANCE	- Authoritarian	- Liberal-Democratic
RULE OF LAW	- Inequity of Justice; Impunity & Corruption	- Equity of Justice; Accountability
GOVERNMENTAL SERVICES	- As Private Commodities	- As Public Goods

Table 1. The Winners and Losers of Growing U.S. Inequality

The Winners

The benefactors of rising inequality within the U.S. are those individuals, organizations, entities, and ideologies that either exist in the wealthiest segments of society, benefit from its existence and are representative of it, or have learned to adjust their economic strategies to target their goods, services, and capital allocation strategies to high end and lower end markets. Individuals and entities that have shown themselves to be productive (functional) in 5th dimensional technologies and know how to operate within the sovereign free and illicit segments of the globalized economy—such as those concentrated in Silicon Valley and other technical hubs—have also prospered. The 'winners' of rising inequality within the U.S. are as follows:

- *The Upper Classes*: In many ways, we are still haunted by Percy Shelly's well known early 19th century adage 'The rich get richer and the poor get poorer' and its forgotten and prophetic later segment 'and the vessel of the State is driven between the Scylla and Charybdis of anarchy and despotism' which resonates with contemporary U.S. domestic relations.[111] In fact, those at the highest income levels continue to gain the most benefits now that 20th century state moderated capitalism is in its twilight, if not all but dead. This is underscored by data provided in an earlier section of this work and the fact that, in 1980, the top 1% of Americans had 10% of the total income which grew to 20% in 2016 while the bottom 50% of Americans saw their income fall from 20% of the total in 1980 to 13% in 2016. Such growing income discrepancies are partially due to ongoing changes to the U.S. tax code that favor the richer economic strata.[112]

- *Multinational Corporations*: The days of deep mutual interests between the U.S. and large corporations embodied in this statement by GM's CEO, Charles

Wilson during his 1953 confirmation hearing for Secretary of Defense—"I thought what was good for the country was good for General Motors and vice versa"— have long since left us.[113] This corporation, like its brethren, operates in a world of migratory global capital seeking the highest returns on investment achievable. If this results in pulling car manufacturing out of Detroit and turning it into a rusting and decaying façade of itself or closing down the steel mills in Pittsburg (which had existed for a century and a half as a component of American industrialization) for a couple % points of profit so be it.[114] This has resulted in a gradual 'Power Shift' per Jessica Mathews taking place over the course of decades that has witnessed multinationals increasing in power relative to nation-states and even playing them off against each other in order to cut the most lucrative corporate deals.[115]

- *Informational-Internet Technology Based Big Business:* High tech internet, cloud, and computer focused companies such as Google, Apple, Facebook, Ebay, and Amazon—and also informational leveraging financial companies such Goldman Sachs and Bloomberg—have achieved great wealth from the information revolution. Their small cadres of skilled knowledge workers and traders earn some of the highest salary levels in the world.[116] Additionally, niche businesses targeting the "Tiffany's" and "Dollar General" economic dichotomy (for example, those in our earlier Bay area and Stilwell examples, respectively) are also prospering along with retailers who are 'data driven' such as Walmart, Costco, and IKEA. Walmart, however, as part of its stellar success has resulted in countless small town business closures across America while paying its employees what have been considered 'poverty wages' in the process. Further, when incremental wage increases do take place, they are viewed as being disingenuous and politically motivated.[117] 'Big Law' firms with offices spread throughout the globe and relying increasingly upon AI-powered software for multinational corporation case support should also be considered winners vis-a-vis growing levels of inequality.[118]

- *Sovereign Free & Illicit Economies (Non-Taxable):* As the formal economy in America gets compressed—along with that of the middle class—revenues and profits are being pushed into the sovereign free and illicit economies. An example of sovereign free revenues would be the use of tax havens by corporations operating in the U.S.[119] One estimate suggests that the U.S. loses "…close to $70 billion a year in tax revenue due to the shifting of corporate profits to tax havens. That's close to 20 percent of the corporate tax revenue that is collected each year."[120] This estimate is in addition to the fact that "…an estimated $8.7 trillion, 11.5 percent of the entire world's GDP, is held offshore by ultrawealthy households in a handful of tax shelters, and most of it isn't being reported to the relevant tax authorities."[121] At the middle and other end of the economic spectrum, the value of the unreported earnings (including illicit income) in the U.S. in 2009 was estimated to be in the $1.8-$2.4 trillion range, resulting in a $390 to $537 billion annual tax gap.[122] The illicit component of these earnings is fully out of reach of public taxation and in fact requires large law enforcement, judicial, and corrections expenditures to be made in order to suppress it.[123] Unsurprisingly, an increasing trend has taken place within individual states (Colorado, California, Washington, et.al.)—cash starved for revenue and overburdened with 'light drug use' convictions—to legalize marijuana production, distribution, and sales for much needed revenue purposes.[124] This is reminiscent of state promoted lotteries to cash in on the gambling habits of their citizenry. Both forms of legalization seek to reach into the illicit economy, recast certain activities as socially acceptable, and make them taxable as a component of the formal economy.

- *Polarizing Elites & Fringe Factions:* Single-issue interest groups, the political fringe, and politicians who cater to their vote are also the benefactors of rising inequality within our society. As public resources become more and more scarce, a visceral 'too many rats in the cage and not enough food' mentality is permeating American politics. Extremely nasty narratives and a lack of civility is evident on both the political left and right now, with Antifa (anti-fascist) and white supremacy groups engaging in occasional street battles and urban (and more liberal) America and rural (and more conservative) America increasingly disenfranchised from one another. A recent study suggests that progressive activists comprising 8% of the population on the left and traditional and devoted conservatives comprising 19% and 6% on the right, respectively, have resulted in political tribal conflict breaking out over core beliefs. These partisan wings within American society are far more politically engaged that the exhausted mainstream voters with polarizing politicians, news pundits, and other elites who know how to energize them reaping governmental offices and other political and economic rewards.[125] Each of the fringe factions of American society (i.e. hidden tribes) "…have a shared set of beliefs, values, and identities that shape the way they see the world."[126] Of concern is that with war increasingly being fought over 'future social and political organization' as a component of the epochal change process—see the next section of this work—we may now be witnessing the beginnings of such epochal conflict taking place domestically.

- *Authoritarian Governance*: Donald Trump's ascension to the White House has become a highly contentious affair, portending a shift to a new form of direct and open conflict in political affairs. Still, his election to office should be considered an outcome of growing inequality and societal class stresses on America rather than their initial causation. The current president is a non-apologetic, highly self assured, and extremely wealthy individual who has more in common with elites than with common Americans—and the latter is not in itself new to the office. The core problem, however, lies in his style of governance—based on a career of high level business dealings (e.g. *The Art of the Deal*)—which is inherently authoritarian in its approach, seeking to permanently discredit any opposition.[127] If this approach to governance becomes an outlier or a new pattern for the future remains unknown but the failure to grasp the necessity of checks and balances in American governance to inhibit the rise of despotic tyranny and the accepted inefficiencies that come with it built into the Constitution could have permanent and serious repercussions. Further, the willingness to unabashedly engage with authoritarian and blatantly undemocratic leaders without some semblance of disapproval bodes poorly for the upholding of American values as sacrosanct.

- *Inequity of Justice; Impunity & Corruption:* As societies become polarized between the 'haves' and the 'have nots,' impunity for the elites increasingly exists and corruption—which directly results in providing economic benefits to a small segment of our populace—begins to eat away within private companies and public institutions. In 2007-2008, the 19 biggest banks reportedly gave out $80 billion in dividends at the same time as they drew $160 billion in bailout funds from the U.S. Treasury and even more from the Fed's emergency lending fund while the bottom 99% never recovered their losses from the crash.[128] The impunity socialization process can readily be seen in the way in which children of the elite get special considerations at expensive private colleges—from bending the rules for admittance through getting slapped on the wrist for the use of cocaine or public drunkenness—while, at a working class public university, arrest and expulsion would likely follow.[129] Failing a slap on the wrist, the scions of the elite can have the scales of justice tipped in their favor for enough money—a first time drunk driving offense can be made to essentially go away if a high powered lawyer is retained.[130] The child of a poor family would find no such economic redemption and would face the full brunt of the law that would likely include mandatory jail time. Governmental corruption examples also abound including partisan gerrymandering, the shutting down of polling places, striking registered voters from rolls, and even now a U.S. governmental official firing an investigator looking into their own malfeasance.[131]

- *Governmental Services as Private Commodities:* The intent of the upper classes who seek sovereign-free status is to privatize goods and services provided for by the state to its citizenry. The reason for this is that such high net worth individuals do not utilize public schools for the education of their children, substitute gated communities and armed private security guards in order to protect their homes and neighborhoods instead of relying upon local police forces, and utilize their own personal doctors for their family's health care needs. These 1%-ers would never dream of utilizing public transportation such as a bus line, visiting a local public library, or taking a class at a community center. Public goods are useless to the elite within society because they have commoditized them.[132] From a cost-benefit perspective, they are economically much better off if their income and capital gains taxes levels are reduced even if this results in the state being 'hollowed out' in the process. On the reverse side, citizens living in economically depressed areas will look to the collective security offered by local street gangs who represent a 24 hour security presence rather than over burdened law enforcement officers, with response times for some calls taking hours.

The Losers

Those individuals, groups, and entities suffering from rising U.S. inequality—such as blue-collar workers and middle management, labor union employees, retirees with a secure pension, and the traditional industries within which they were employed—as well as the two party system that long dominated domestic politics, are quickly becoming historical anachronisms with their time in the sun quickly passing. Rising inequality has resulted in many more economic 'losers' than 'winners.' While unemployment is presently at historically low national levels, the majority of jobs being generated are low-paying with minimal benefits—in fact, middle-wage jobs are declining— befitting a middle class falling into servant economy status.[133] The economic losers of the early 21st century within America are:

- *The Lower & Middle Classes*: It has been plainly evident throughout this document that the lower and middle classes are economically suffering within the U.S. on all measures of inequality; wages and net assets found in such measures as the Gini coefficient, quintile analysis, essential good purchases, and poverty lines. While a beggar on the street of an American urban center earning $10 USD a day might be considered part of the 'great global middle class' that has emerged, this is not a survivable income within American society. To add insult to injury, a high priced lawyer makes far more money selling a day's worth of their labor than such a global middle class designated individual would do during the course of an entire year. Where marked inequality is readily evident is found in life expectancy differentials of up to 20 years between the upper and lower classes within the U.S.[134] Further, according to a University of Washington study, "America's 'life expectancy gap' is also predicted to grow even wider in future, with 11.5% of U.S. counties having experienced an increase in the risk of death for residents aged 25–45 over the period studied (1980-2014). No previous study has put the disparity at even close to 20 years."[135] This increasing lifespan gap between the rich and poor—and those within the middle class falling into poverty—is due to lack of access to quality health care and insurance (a social good the federal government is attempting to eliminate) and lifestyle vices such as smoking, drinking, and drug use (components of predatory economies) which correlates with lower educational and socio-economic levels. Recent record heat waves which have resulted in the deaths of elderly and health-compromised individuals who were unable to afford air conditioning further shows the vulnerability of these populations.[136]

- *Local-to-National Companies*: Globalization is favoring transnational and niche overseas manufacturing concerns—many engaging in off-the-books and after hours production runs—at the expense of small through somewhat larger U.S. business concerns. Further, with the shift in the economy, traditional entities such as small book and hardware stores, florists, travel agents, and other middle class service related industries are fading away. This trend has not gone unnoticed— "According to Gallup's CEO, more businesses are dying than being created in the United States for the first time starting in 2009 and continuing on."[137] Along with this trend, American entrepreneurship itself is declining as millennials have an inability to afford the costs of a start up due to individual college debt levels and lack of homeownership (from which to borrow funds), the time-consuming sacrifices it requires, the fact that major corporations are buying up patents and other forms of intellectual property at an increasing rate, and since technology—such as AI—is making the ideas of individual inventors and garage startups increasingly irrelevant.[138] This inability to engage in small business entrepreneurship further contributes to members of the lower classes being unable to improve their socio-economic station within society and perpetuates ongoing levels of inequality.

- *Industrial Technology and Brick & Mortar Based Businesses:* The loss of non-competitive U.S. industrial age industries—with their well-paying union jobs—to mass closures and offshoring represented one of the initial shocks to the U.S. middle class beginning in the 1980s. Along with the legacy of the 'rust belt' appearing across the former manufacturing regions of the U.S. came other shocks with the addition of the flattening of organizational structures by information technologies eliminating the need for middle management rungs and corporate raiders (of the 'Gordon Gekko' *Wall Street* archetype) coming in to break up companies which had more value in the sum of their parts than as ongoing and profitable business entities comprised of employees with families to feed. A wave of mall and small business closures also came as multinational corporations such as WalMart spread into medium size towns across the U.S. Even today, we are witnessing a new round of brick and mortar U.S. business institutions such as JC Penny (slowly imploding), Sears (now in bankruptcy), and Toys R Us (defunct) going under as their middle class clients are economically being forced to boycott them for cheaper online and mass produced (via China) big box goods. While some hope existed that under the present administration U.S. jobs would once again be 're-shored' domestically, this will not be the case. Instead, robotic 'no shoring' is expected with labor costs being saved by the implementation of full scale factory automation.[139]

- *Formal Economy (Taxable):* Few realize that 'papal infallibility' (the Catholic dogma stemming from divine revelation and Petrine supremacy) as a spiritual gift would have some similarity to neoclassical economic—that is to say, today's extremely influential Chicago School—tenets. Just as the Pope can do no wrong, 'the efficiency of free markets' has also been imbued with an ethereal form of charism that we must place our faith within. While the "reduction or elimination of regulations on business" may sound like the pinnacle of laissez-faire achievement, it allows for highly predatory and ultra-efficient forms of capitalism to emerge outside of liberal-democratic state moderation.[140] As a result, the formal—read state taxable—economy suffers as unfettered capitalism strives for the highest returns possible by logically removing itself either outside of (illicitly) or beyond the realm of state authority (through extra-sovereign means).

- *Democratic and Republican Moderates:* The American political system as an archetype should be thought of as a 'great political pendulum' that swings right and left, distributing laws, polices, and public goods to our citizenry. The expectation is that all segments along the continuum of political affiliation from the right to the left will be represented and receive governmental goods and services. This process is meant to keep the vast majority of our population franchised with a vested and ongoing stake in the nation and its future wellbeing.

This bi-partisan approach to political affiliation (with occasional 3rd party challenges) has traditionally defined the American party system with centrists from both sides of the spectrum reaching compromises for national benefit.[141] Following this 'pendulum logic,' neither party should dominate the executive office and the two chambers of Congress for extended periods of time. In this way, the national electoral swing to right and then to the left and then back again continues as a mass political enfranchisement balance is maintained. This process has increasingly been thrown into disarray with moderates from both parties leaving Congress, incivility becoming more pronounced as partisanship increases, and compromises reached for the common good failing to be made.[142] Without a moderating elected middle (and the required centrist voters who have fled the Democratic and Republican parties to vote them into office), the bi-partisan political pendulum is starting to move in a jerky fashion from one extreme to the other, increasingly benefiting fringe special interests.

- *Independents (Opt Outs):* As more American voters—especially the younger generations (tail-end Xers and millennials)—become disenfranchised with the political process in the United States, we are seeing the growth of an opted out 'ghost party.' It is presently estimated that 42% of Americans identify themselves as independent voters. This represents a block of voters larger in number than either of the two major parties, respectively.[143] This hodgepodge assortment of voters does not have a political voice like the traditional Democratic and Republican parties and can be viewed as a post-modern development, indicative of the ongoing early

21ˢᵗ century thinning of the middle class and the loss of societal consensus that goes with it. Independents' anti-partisanship, however, does not translate into a viable near-term centrist party emerging. Rather, American democracy has become dysfunctional with the traditional platforms of the dominant parties— whose narratives related to fiscal conservancy and support of labor versus management are becoming very difficult to pin down—are no longer in sync with the majority of voters.[144]

- *Liberal-Democratic Governance:* "In war, truth is the first casualty," according to the 5ᵗʰ century BC dramatist Aeschylus.[145] If this is the case, then surely the barrage of 'fake news' (i.e. propaganda statements) being generated by the left and right fringes in American politics and from the authoritarian governments of Vladimir Putin's Russia and Xi Jinping's China surely suggest that a global conflict between liberal-democracy on one side and internal 'we win, you lose' factions and despotic regimes on the other is underway. While we had hoped that the information revolution and globalization would be a boon to democratic and Western interests—and which initially appeared to be the case—authoritarian information counter-operations are now in full swing outside of our country while fringe-based ones are actively being promoted domestically. With much of the West's attention focused on countering radical Islamist extremist narratives related to al Qaeda, the Islamic State, and affiliated groups, we have ignored until quite recently the whispering voices of the domestic fringe and foreign authoritarianism. The intent of such narratives is to both undermine democratic values at home while seeking to overthrow the global economic and political order (including alliance networks such as NATO and SEATO) established by America after the Second World War.[146] Tragically, from our own White House, we have even now been subjected to a steady barrage of Tweets that promote a narrative of fear and internal division—instead of measured optimism and national cohesion—based on pronouncements not grounded in any factual basis but rather derived from populist rhetoric and sound bites. It has been noted that "the opinions of the poor may be the most uncertain and susceptible to opinion manipulation" such that misinformation may "even give rise to a form of false consciousness."[147] On the other hand, the more affluent are better able to convert their resources into political influence, especially through campaign contributions, subverting the true essence of democracy.[148]

- *Equity of Justice; Accountability:* As corruption and impunity worms its way into the American body politic and the corporate boardroom—even more so than would be expected at the margins—the societal ideal that equity of justice exists for all citizens and that those who engage in wrongdoing, betrayal of the public trust, and illicit practices will ultimately be ferretted out, arrested, convicted, and harshly sentenced for their crimes begins to erode.[149] While in the lesser developed countries of Latin America—Mexico and Colombia being but two examples—*¿Plato O Plomo?* (Silver or Lead) is the dominant form of narco promoted intimidation utilized to achieve impunity, in the U.S., the more refined plutocratic approach, *¿Plato O Abogado?* (Silver or Lawyer) seems a more appropriate description of how the criminal and civil justice system is circumvented.

Still, from the illicit economy side, the Federal Bureau of Investigation (FBI) has sent up 49 Border Corruption Task Forces focusing on public corruption concerns to ensure that societal trust in local government and law enforcement operations is maintained.[150] Such activity, however, can be juxtaposed with the simultaneously calling into question of the integrity of the FBI by the executive branch of the Federal government—itself under special investigation— and the tainting of the legitimacy of the Supreme Court Justice confirmation process.[151]

- *Governmental Services as Public Goods:* As less monies come into the U.S. Treasury due to a) corporate and high end earner tax cuts, b) profitable areas of the economy increasingly escaping taxation by becoming—legally through avoidance (due to extra-sovereign but legal ploys) and illegally through evasion (due to tax cheating and money laundering)—beyond revenue collection, and c) yearly public debt interest servicing (representing approximately 7.4% of all the FY18 federal budget outlays and increasing) less public goods will be available for the citizenry.[152] Interest servicing on the national public debt is projected to jump into the 12% range in 2023, at which point it may pass up Medicaid expenses making it the 3rd largest governmental expenditure after Social Security, defense spending, and Medicare.[153] One recent proposal to help balance the federal budget—post the 2017 H.R.1 - Tax Cuts and Jobs Act—which lowered taxes for the American elites is to now, not surprisingly, target Medicare, Medicaid, and Social Security for massive federal cost saving cuts which would further serve to exacerbate inequality levels related to public goods and services provision (increasingly privatized) within our nation.[154] An area of public good degradation already taking place nationally is in the corrections (i.e. prison) sector where mass incarceration over the last three decades has led to the rise of 'for profit' prisons and related predatory economic practices targeting those who are incarcerated.[155]

For U.S. society in general and 'America's Army' (which is meant to be representative of it) in particular, a more bifurcated society as described above likely will result in the development of ideological inconsistencies. The oath of military service requires that service personnel "support and defend the Constitution of the United States" which forms the basis of our system of liberal-democratic governance but, increasingly, the legal interpretation of that Constitution is and will likely continue being called into question. As these interpretations drift from long-held standards and as the armed services themselves shift in form and mission, it may become increasingly difficult for troops to be certain they still protect our founding constitutional values. The Army has long been a preserve for those values. It is held that after World War II it was the G.I. Bill that provided for the education and training allowing former servicemen to become America's burgeoning middle class. [156] A move from a mass industrialized and nationalistic army (e.g. Modern)—of and for the people—to a smaller and more professionally based informational army (e.g. post-Modern), however, may result in new narratives more in line with the interests of our elites. There is an early 20th century precedent. In the words of Marine General Smedley Butler:

> "I spent 33 years and four months in
> active military service and during that period
> I spent most of my time as a high class muscle

man for Big Business, for Wall Street and the
bankers. In short, I was a racketeer, a gangster
for capitalism."[157]

Back when Butler was fighting for American capitalism,
it extracted wealth primarily from the rest of the world and
brought it home domestically. Ultimately subordinated to our
national interest, it subsequently allowed for both the middle
and lower classes to greatly prosper later in the 20th century.
This time around, however, the new strain of globalized
capitalism that has emerged will not be so easily moderated by
the state—no 'Trust Busters' of the likes of Roosevelt or Taft
exist on the distant horizon. Further, the economic carnage
resulting this time around includes a growing component of
American society—the increasingly disenfranchised economic
'losers' mentioned above.[158]

V

Theoretical Constructs Related
to Rising Inequality

The initial sections of this manuscript have focused upon increasing levels of global, Western, and domestic inequality and the gradual evisceration of the middle class within our society and what this means for both societal cohesion and the social mobility prospects of its poorer socio-economic elements. Income and wealth data interpreted by Gini coefficients, quintiles, and related analytical measurements support these contentions while the preceding section highlights the winners and losers within American society stemming from a new form of predatory and globalized capitalism that has emerged. It can be recognized that this new form of capitalism is in direct variance to the older state moderated capitalism that was more conducive to liberal-democratic values and institutions. These perceptions and insights on their own, however, are insufficient to properly comprehend the greater strategic significant that rising levels of inequality within the U.S. and the subsequent compression of the middle class in our society portends for our nation's future. Such comprehension can only be gained by placing these events in their broader qualitative state-form and historical context. In order to do, we must view rising inequality contextually—through the analytical lens of what is known as Fourth Epoch theory. Set at the macro-theoretical level of analysis, the epochal change paradigm focuses on the civilizational shift from the modern to the post-modern era and the incipient—as well as the longer-term—implications this will have upon the security posture and institutional integrity of the United States.

The epochal change paradigm was first developed in 1987 by one of the authors in collaboration with T. Lindsay Moore and utilizes qualitative historical modeling to posit that two epochal shifts have previously taken place within Western civilization (from the Classical to the Medieval and then from the Medieval to the Modern) with a third shift presently underway.[159] The utility of this construct was initially hindered by lack of contemporary data point collaboration but, over the ensuing thirty-years time, has increasingly been validated—though it still remains little known outside of selective international and domestic security and defense policy academic and professional circles. The paradigm can be considered allied to and synergistic with such works as Hedley Bull's *The Anarchical Society* (1977)—emphasizing the rise of a new medievalism as states recede; Martin van Creveld's *The Transformation of War* (1991)—focusing on violent non-state actor ascendancy over institutionalized state militaries; Phillip Bobbitt's *Shield of Achilles* (2002)—which proposes market state variants (e.g. entrepreneurial, mercantile, and managerial) are emerging as a successor to the modern state form; and Nils Gilman et. al.'s *Deviant Globalization* (2011)—which explores the 'other' vital component of the global economy which is amoral, satisfies demand for illicit goods and services, and allows for the world's poor to engage in wealth creation.[160] These works, and many related ones, were highlighted within a chapter from a political economy work in 2015 on the present epochal transition—termed a 'Dark Renaissance'—now underway.[161]

To understand what this transition will likely mean for inequality in the U.S., a short discussion on epochal civilizations is required to provide some context. Each civilizational period—per the epochal change model—manifests its own unique and distinctive socio-economic and technologic characteristics that the dominant state form is configured upon. Within the context of this essay, our analytical interest rests both within each civilizational period (i.e., the Classical, the Medieval, and the Modern) when 'wars of efficiency' take place and during the transitions between them when 'wars of destiny' take place. These transitions—representative of civilizational shifts and concurrent state form deinstitutionalization—witness the demise of the older form of 'social and political organization' (including its dominant military structures) and the eventual rise of a new one better configured to the socio-economic and technologic requirements of a more advanced level of human civilization.

With regard to Western civilizational periods, three are identified as having existed with two—the Classical and Medieval eras—representative of earlier historical periods and one—the Modern era—representative of our contemporary world. A fourth era—the still emergent Post-Modern era—representative of a new civilizational period has also been articulated within this model based on projected estimates (See Table 2.). Each civilizational period has its own unique structural attributes derived from the energy foundation that is configured upon. The Classical era was founded on human energy, saw the rise of the city state form with the Roman Empire representing its pinnacle achievement, and witnessed two infantry articulations—first the phalanx and later the legion—with warfighting taking place in two dimensional space based on line (x physical space) combat modified by time (t). The Medieval era was configured around animal energy, resulted in the feudal state form, birthed the Holy Roman Empire and powerful medieval states in France and England, and saw the mounted knight and feudal array supported by patchworks of fiefs and castle strongholds. Medieval forces fought in three-dimensional space based on battlefields (x, y physical space) modified by time (t). The Modern era was founded on mechanical energy—initially machine based, with a later engine based sequence developing—which resulted in the emergence of dynastic states that transitioned into modern nation-states. Military articulations utilizing missile weapons (gunpowder based) evolved from early clockwork-like absolutist army organizations in mass industrial formations, utilizing increasingly powerful artillery and missile systems and armored formations which waged war in four dimensional battlespace (x, y, z physical space) modified by time (t). State political forms during these civilizational eras—city states, feudal states, and nation-states, respectively—engaged in within-paradigm 'wars of efficiency' that focused on better exploiting each respective civilizational era's energy foundation than their competitors.[162]

EPOCH (ENERGY BASIS)	STATE FORM (EXAMPLES)	ARMY STRUCTURE (DIMENSIONALITY)	ECONOMY / IDEOLOGICAL PARADIGM	CLASS STRUCTURE
I: Classical (Human)	City State (Athens, Sparta, Rome)	Infantry Based; Phalanx, Legion (2 Dimensional)	Slave Holding/ Virtue	Slaves Freemen (Owners)
EPOCHAL SHIFT				
II: Medieval (Animal)	Feudal State (Holy Roman Empire, Norman England, Capet & Valois France)	Cavalry Based; Knights & Retainers (3 Dimensional)	Manorialism/ Divine Providence	Serfs (Work) Clergy (Pray) Lords (Fight)
EPOCHAL SHIFT				
III: Modern (Mechanical)	Nation State (France, Germany, England, Japan, U.S.)	Artillery Based; Mass Industrial Armies (4 Dimensional)	Capitalism / Utility	Lower Class Middle Class Upper Class
EPOCHAL SHIFT				
IV: Post-Modern (Post-Mechanical; Electrical)	*Regional or Civilizational State (EU, China, India, North America)*	*Directed Energy; AI-Robotics-Networks (5 Dimensional)*	*Knowledge-Automation/ Cybernetic Interface*	*Lower Class (Non-Augmented) Upper Class (Augmented)*

Table 2. Epochal Change and Class Structure[163]

With regard to contemporary rising inequality in the U.S. (and the greater Western world itself), the attributes of the economy, ideological paradigm, and class structure of each civilizational era are of greatest relevance. The economy of Greece, Rome, and the rest of the Mediterranean world during the Classical era rested upon slavery in order to exploit cheap human energy for initially small scale and later larger (latifundia based) agricultural production. Slaves were also utilized as household servants, as war galley rowers, and for fodder in gladiatorial games in Roman arenas throughout the republic and later empire. Slave holding is thus considered the economic basis of the civilization, with slave and freemen (owners) classes defining its basic class structure with virtue—moral excellence embodied in stoicism, valor, and other qualities of life—embodying its ideological underpinnings. For a slave, the greatest honor was to achieve their independence by means of being freed by their master or by winning it in the arena for their success in the gladiatorial games.

The economy of the Medieval era, in turn, was based upon manorialism—the raising of animals (most importantly, war horses) on feudal estates by nobles linked to one another by a system of vassalage—with serfs bound to the land working it. Within the social class structure, lords who owned the land and fought as knights, supported by their retainers, and clergy who dedicated their lives to the universal church comprised the rest of it. Divine providence (God's will) based upon monotheism (replacing Classical Greco-Roman polytheism) provided the ideological perspective of this civilization, with each social class accepting their place in the chain of being in this life while looking forward to eternal salvation and the blessings of eternal paradise in the next.

Finally, the economy of the Modern era is based upon increasingly industrialized capitalism, that is, initially mercantilist in orientation (machine based) and with higher levels of capitalism (steam and gasoline internal combustion based) developing later. A robust middle class gradually developed out of the old Medieval guild structures and factory floors of the late 18th and early 19th centuries as industrial production flourished and modern welfare (social) state principles took hold. This resulted in the production of mass goods and services and the fielding of large scale national armies numbering in the millions of personnel—both of which require a healthy and vibrant middle class. With the separation of church and state in the West came an ideological system configured around utility with its notions of profitability and beneficiality.

This brings into question what the Post-Modern civilizational era and the social class structure it manifests may someday look like. A projection of the defining structures of this civilizational era suggest first and foremost that it will be configured around post-mechanical energy, specifically requiring immense electrical power generation levels, to allow for the proper operation of the offensive and defensive directed energy weaponry (e.g. rail guns, lasers, high powered microwaves, energy walls and shielding) now being developed. The post-modern state form presently appearing seems to be at the regional or civilizational level equivalent to the territorial and population size of the European Union, China, India, and North America. As aforementioned, directed energy will form the basis of the weaponry of the military articulations of this post-modern state form with artificial intelligence (AI), robotics, and networks representing significant components of it. Warfare will be waged in five dimensional battlespace (x, y, z physical space) modified by time (t) and the inclusion of cyberspace (c; informationally) / hyperspace (h; geometrically) to overcome earlier four dimensional (space-time) limitations.

Where this projection becomes 'dark'—from the perspective of a healthy and vibrant U.S. middle class structure and the limited levels of social inequality that accompany it—squarely relates to the attributes of the economy, ideological paradigm, and the ensuing class structure that may well exist. The economic foundations of the Post-Modern era appear to be forming around knowledge and automation interlinked with additive (3D & 4D) manufacturing (resulting in 'post-scarcity' scenarios) which are at variance with the economic tenets of capitalism and industrialization. Just as in late stage Modern era militaries—increasingly bereft of mass industrial armies with the U.S. force structure a prime example—we are also seeing Post-Modern warfare components emerging (which include the fielding of armed robotic systems) which will, even more so, require less of our present middle class structure to support our future warfighting requirements. A similar situation will also take place concerning a new and advanced form of economic production as no requirement for a sizeable middle class will exist to support it.[164] Historically, social classes have risen and fallen, expanded and collapsed over the course of the civilizational eras found within the West. Social classes exist only due to their functionality to economic production and warfighting within a social and political (e.g. state) form. Once that functionality disappears—especially in both areas—the expectation is that a social class will increasingly begin to not only thin out but also lose its political voice and influence.

A further concern exists—from the modernist and traditionalist perspective of the authors—that the new ideological paradigm may shift from one based upon utility to one relating to cybernetic interface. Success and self-identity would be defined by one's network influence and access, interactive potentials, and other enhanced cybernetic capabilities. Such an ideology would go hand-in-glove with a projected social class structure of a non-augmented lower class and an augmented upper class incorporating varying degrees of wetware, bio-implants, and genome therapies that have the potential for increased longevity, associated physical and mental modifications, and network, cyber, and, possibly even, AI interfaces.[165] While such projections may seem more the realm of science fiction, the fact is that already today wetware is increasingly being implanted in human beings and the U.S. military (as well as that of the Chinese) while other advanced states, are engaged in work related to such bio convergence and brain-computer interfaces.[166] Collateral trends to such dystopian perceptions are humanity's rising population levels—now estimated to be well above 7.5 billion people—and increasing urbanization with about 1 billion people (projected to triple by 2050) now living in the teeming slums of the world's megacities and whom are increasingly locked out from ever participating in the formal (i.e. legitimate) global economy.[167]

These vanishing middle class, increased inequality, and excess humanity theoretical 'doom and gloom' potentials, however, are not set in stone. Epochal change is a gradual process that typically takes place over the course of many generations. While we cannot 'fight the future' in terms of the cutting edge capabilities that will continue to unfold, we do still have the capacity to shape it. The time spans of previous epochal shifts have historically taken a century or more. For example, the initial one signifying the transition from the Classical to the Medieval eras, extended from the Battle of Adrianople in 378—which saw the legion vanquished from the battlefield by Gothic cavalry forces—to the Battle of Tours in 732—which saw the establishment of European heavy cavalry to combat the raider threat. The next epochal shift, signifying the transition from the Medieval to the Modern eras, spanned the Battle of Crécy in 1346—which saw an early example of medieval knights being defeated by foot soldiers armed with missile weapons— to the Siege of Constantinople in 1453—which saw the initial success of modern heavy artillery over medieval fortifications.[168] These transitional periods, also known as 'wars of destiny,' are fought over which emerging social and political form— utilizing the new energy foundation developing—would replace the older civilizational one. The initial epochal transition was characterized as the 'Dark Ages' in Europe—external raiders laid waste to the former lands of the Western Roman Empire—while the second transition—characterized as a 'Renaissance'—saw the rebirth of learning in Europe. However, while earlier periods of epochal change took well over a century to take place, the present shift is projected to transpire over a much shorter timespan. This is due to increased 'historical temporal compression' taking place in Western society since the early-to-mid 1800s, with each decade witnessing heightened rates of technological advancement and ensuing social adaption. Few would argue with the perception that, over the course of just one generation, the world of 1998 looked vastly different from our world of today—with the phenomenal growth of the global internet and the worldwide web, broad use of social media seeing billions of people interacting within cyberspace via their smart phones, driverless cars being tested on our highways, and small drones increasingly flying overhead. Accompanying political and military elements of such epochal shifts—with current 'data point' examples suggesting that a new transition is now taking place—include:

- *Dominant State Form Fragility and Failure*—Presently, almost two-hundred nations (at least in name) exist globally with almost forty of them residing at the 'alert' through 'very high alert' levels and about thirty more residing at both the slightly less threatening 'high warning' and 'elevated warning' levels on the State Fragility (formerly State Failure) index in 2017. It would thus be fair to state that nearly half of the world's states are presently exhibiting great levels of structural stress and possess limited institutional capacity. Additionally, euphemisms and methodological approaches may be beginning to obfuscate the critical situation some of these states presently exist within. Libya, for instance, with no central government and warring factions at each other's throats (including a sizable Islamic State fighter contingent) is merely considered on 'alert' concerning its fragility (i.e. failure potentials).[169]

- *The Blurring of Crime and War*—Over the course of some decades, the internal domestic policing and law enforcement environment (which is crime focused) and the external military environment (which is war focused) addressed by state institutions have increasingly blurred. This gray area or 'crime wars' environment represents an operational capability gap for police and law enforcement, which have had to become more military-like (i.e. SWAT and tactical officer emergence), and for the military, which have had to become more police-like (i.e. stability and support focused), in order to contend with it.

- *The Rise of Violent Non-State Actors*—rural guerrillas have evolved into urban guerrillas and then later emerged as politically and then religiously inspired terrorists. At the same time, organized criminal groups of one variety or another—including mafias, drug cartels, human traffickers, pirates, and street and prison gangs—have spread and flourished. Early Khat chewing technicals in Somalia, mujahidin in Afghanistan, and gangsters on the streets of Los Angeles have now given way to a bewildering array of heavily armed insurgents, sicarios, and foreign fighters that mix criminality with terrorist actions for secular, ideological, and religious imperatives.

- *The Return of Mercenaries to the Battlefield*—Private security, armed contractor, and mercenary employment on both the world's battlefields and on the streets of its cities for private policing purposes have reached security privatization (i.e. as a commodity not as a public good) levels not seen since the Renaissance/initial phase of the Early Modern period. Contemporary mercenary and private security corporations include Executive Outcomes, Blackwater (later called Xe and Academi), Triple Canopy, the Wagner Group, and Frontier Services Group.

- *Advanced Weaponry Emergence*—There is an increasing shift from gunpowder and mechanical based weaponry (i.e. firearms and explosive devices—bombs and missiles) under direct human control to directed energy weapons (i.e. lasers, microwaves, and software programs) and armed droids and drones which are semi- and fully-autonomous, increasingly with artificial intelligence (AI) network capability.

- *The Development of Advanced Battlespace*—The inclusion of a 5th dimensional attribute—identified as cyberspace (c; for its informational expression) / hyperspace (h; for its geometric expression)—to modern four-dimensional battlespace composed of three-dimensional (x, y, z) space and time (t). Increasingly mature 5th dimensional warfighting capabilities will include the ability to bypass and defeat traditional tank armor with out of phase weaponry and the projection of energy barriers and shields for defensive purposes.

- *New Forms of Warfare Considered Anathema to Contemporary Laws and Norms*—The condemnation of the advanced weaponry and approaches to warfare ushered in via the emergent civilization by the institutions and vested interests of the older civilization which view them as an existential challenge to their ethical, ideological, and legalistic foundations and underlying power structures. Examples include 'blinding laser bans' and campaigns to stop 'killer robots' and 'weaponized AI' as well as the United States' inability to initially recognize or even now effectively contend with Russia's weaponization of global social media for political warfare purposes.

Derived from this paradigm, globalization itself can be placed within the greater historical context of large-scale migratory activity during epochal shifts. The transition from the Classical to the Medieval era was defined by large scale migrations of various Gothic and Hunnish tribes—and incipient colonization and later looting—throughout the West. In turn, the transition from the Medieval to the Modern era saw the conquest, looting, and colonization of the new world (and the later extension of conquest to the rest of the non-European regions of the globe). The transition from the Modern to the Post-Modern era—within which globalization is presently taking place—is seeing a different form of migratory expression. With no new territories left upon the face of the globe to conquer or colonize, humanity is now colonizing cyberspace (which is representative of a virtual overlay over our physical reality).[170] This virtual overlay has greatly diminished the physical effects of space-time making the 'distant' now 'local' and resulting in the emergence of increasing global economic and informational (and cultural) interdependencies. A pronounced downside of the migration to cyberspace, however, is that, with the merging of the world's once fragmented economies, all the 'economic bathwater' each one once contained are coming together to create a rather tepid mixture. With global economic equilibrium increasingly being reached, no 'Third World' exists for the West to extract wealth from. As a result, the internal looting and extraction of capital is now taking place within a West whose people are now being treated little differently than other global citizens.

With these perceptions in mind, the one component that the epochal change paradigm had been missing for over two decades was a mechanism that convincingly portrayed the 'compression process' (earlier described as 'a chemical process in a crucible') related to state form deconstruction.[171] The key to unlocking this process was found in the 1993 insurgency futures writings of Steven Metz—presently the director of research, SSI USAWC—by focusing on his commercial insurgency construct.[172] He posited that "Two forms of insurgency are likely to dominate the post-cold war world"—spiritual insurgency and commercial insurgency.[173] Specific observations by Metz concerning the latter form are as follows:

> This will be driven less by the desire for justice than wealth. Its psychological foundation is a warped translation of Western popular culture which equates wealth, personal meaning, and power...
>
> When the discontented define personal meaning by material possessions rather than psychic fulfillment, they create the environment for commercial insurgency. This was made possible when Western materialism penetrated nearly every corner of the Third World via electronic communications and widespread

travel. Commercial insurgency is a quasi-political distortion of materialism…

The quickest and easiest path to material possessions and the satisfaction they appear to bring is crime. And, since the discontented of the Third World feel little attachment to the dominant system of values in their societies anyway, moral restraints on criminal activity are limited…

In this psychological context, commercial insurgency is essentially widespread and sustained criminal activity with a proto-political dimension that challenges the security of the state. In the modern world, its most common manifestation is narco-insurgency, although it may also be based on other forms of crime, especially smuggling. The defining feature is expansion of the criminal activity into a security threat, especially in the hinterlands where government control is limited.[174]

The above omission related to the process of state deconstruction was partially rectified by John P. Sullivan with his articulation of the 'criminal insurgency' construct in 2008.[175] It was then fully analytically completed by Robert Bunker's development of the 'plutocratic insurgency' construct in 2011, the required complement to Sullivan's articulation.[176] These new constructs draw upon Metz's older commercial insurgency work and apply it to non-state actors who operate within the criminal and sovereign free economies, respectively. Overviews of these two insurgency constructs are as follows.[177]

Criminal Insurgency

This variant of commercial insurgency initially focused on the ongoing narco-conflict in Mexico but has since been expanded to provide other geographic examples. It focuses on criminal enterprises—gangs (specifically 3GEN ones), cartels, and associated mercenary groups (e.g. Los Zetas, et. al.) competing with the state. Members of these enterprises are typically drawn from the lower socio-economic classes and have little to no educational or training skills that would allow them to participate in the formal economy. They grew up in poverty and have suffered high levels of inequality, family dysfunction, and discrimination all their lives—this is their one chance to economically make it. Due to the changing nature of global capitalism, the intent of this criminality, which transcends the symbiotic nature of older forms of organized crime, now seeks to free itself from state control in order to maximize profits from illicit economic activities. Unlike traditional insurgency, this form of insurgency may not be premeditated and was not initially driven by political motivations. Eventual freedom from sovereign rule by such criminal groups, however, results in their *de facto* political control of the cities, towns, and regions under their influence. The Mexican states of Michoacán, Guerrero, and Tamaulipas readily represent examples of this reality.[178] In 2012, Sullivan identified four levels of criminal insurgency which progressively become more and more threatening to a state:

> *Local Insurgencies:* First, criminal insurgencies may exist as 'local insurgencies' in a single neighborhood or 'failed community' where gangs dominate local turf and political,

economic and social life. These areas may be 'no-go zones' avoided by the police. The criminal enterprise collects taxes and exercises a near-monopoly on violence... Here the criminal gang is seeking to develop a criminal enclave or criminal free state. Since the nominal state is never fully supplanted, development of a parallel state is the goal.

Battle for the Parallel State: Second, criminal insurgencies may be battles for control of the 'parallel state.' These occur within the parallel state's governance space, but also spill over to affect the public at large and the police and military forces that seek to contain the violence and curb the erosion of governmental legitimacy and solvency that results. In this case, the gangs or cartels battle each other for domination or control of the criminal enclave or criminal enterprise. The battle between cartels and their enforcer gangs to dominate the 'plazas' is an insurgency where one cartel seeks to replace the other in the parallel state.

Combating the State: Third, criminal insurgencies may result when the criminal enterprise directly engages the state itself to secure or sustain its independent range of action. This occurs when the state cracks down and takes action to dismantle or contain the criminal gang or cartel. In this case, the cartel attacks back. This is the situation seen in Michoacán where La Familia retaliated against the Mexican military and intelligence services in their July 2009 counterattacks. Here the cartels are active belligerents against the state.

The State Implodes: Fourth, criminal insurgency may result when high intensity criminal violence spirals out of control. Essentially this would be the cumulative effect of sustained, unchecked criminal violence and criminal subversion of state legitimacy through endemic corruption and co-option. Here the state simply loses the capacity to respond. This variant has not occurred in Mexico or Central America yet, but is arguably the situation in Guinea-Bissau where criminal entities have transitioned the state into a virtual narco-state. This could occur in other fragile zones if cartel and gang violence is left to fester and grow.[179]

Criminal insurgencies—especially more pronounced ones beyond the local level (where a gang takes over a street, housing project, or neighborhood)—are found in the more fragile states where state institutional capacity is low, the rule of law is compromised or nonexistent, and a middle class strata void indicative of a sizable demographic gap exists between the 'haves' and 'have nots.' These states are defined by their large societal inequalities, sizable informal and criminal economies, and political corruption. Wide swaths of the population are at best ignored and forgotten with few public goods provided to them and at worst exploited, tortured, and killed by criminalized and autocratic governments serving only the interests of powerful individuals and their retainers, alliances of ruling families, and other small privileged enclaves of power.

The criminal insurgency construct was initially met with some resistance and push back from academics, foreign representatives of states suffering the ill effects of this new insurgency form, and polite U.S. governmental officials who don't openly use the 'I' word when describing the security predicament that Mexico and various other states have found themselves in. Research and publication related to this construct is sustained and ongoing—with a number of books and other works out—as more and more scholars and security professionals endorse and publish on this construct.[180] It has now increasingly supplanted more traditionalist organized crime views that posit mafias and other organized criminals do not have the capacity or the intent to kill their host states or end up co-opting and corrupting their institutions—backed by the coercive power of their private armies—to the point that they become their new suzerains.

Plutocratic Insurgency

This other variant of commercial insurgency exists at the opposite end of the spectrum from a criminal and illicit economic based insurgency. In this instance, the "winners of globalization," represented by global elites and multinational corporations, are seeking to remove themselves from the regulatory, taxation, and, ultimately, political authority of states. Why suffer the burdens and duties of state citizenship when one can move beyond them. This is done by promoting an extra-sovereign economy: using foreign tax havens, playing states off against each other to maximize profit, being a nonresident citizen so as not to pay taxes, and employing a bevy of lawyers and lobbyists within states to gain special privileges and economic considerations. This is very much representative of a Gilded Age (1870-1900) redux, but at a globalized level. No sovereign authority presently exists to contend with such an insurgent form, one that is an unintended consequence of globalized capitalism and is resulting in growing economic inequalities within and between Western states—as well as within and between states throughout the globe, yet has been relatively violence free. Some might argue, however, that law enforcement and judicial elements of co-opted states can be "legally utilized" by the plutocratic insurgents to suppress anti-plutocratic protests and demonstrations.[181]

Research and publication on this construct is still somewhat minimal but ongoing.[182] To date, it has only had limited academic and policy impact compared to the far more established and slightly older criminal insurgency construct. This is likely due to the cognitive dissonance this construct portends—for American and Western citizenry, it calls into question their long held world views related to free-trade and capitalism which are foundational to the liberal-democratic order. Highlighting the brutal fact that "Eight Individuals are Now as Wealthy as the Poorest Half of the World" or "69% of Americans Don't Even Have $1,000 in Savings" hits too close to home.[183] It serves to undermine notions of the 'American Dream' derived from a Horatio Alger's ethos that offers its hardworking and industrious citizens the possibility of unlimited prosperity and success.

The construct also has the potential to be dismissed out of hand or at least sullied by allegations that it could be linked to neo-Marxist, anti-capitalist, and Occupy movement (i.e. anarchist) type thinking. Pointing a finger at the most successful, talented, and richest segment of our citizens (and those in other states across the globe) and suggesting that they have now amassed too much wealth and power relative to the rest of American (and global) society seems inherently un-American. The plutocratic insurgency construct, however, is neither anti-capitalist, anti-American, or anti-liberal-democratic. The reverse is in fact true. The underpinnings of our nation and its socio-economic class structure are based on a strong, vibrant, and politically engaged middle class, which also serves to facilitate social mobility. A high Gini coefficient—as is now found in American society—indicates that a widening chasm has appeared between the very rich and the very poor. Lack of opportunities for social advancement—especially for the children of the economically marginalized—ultimately breeds discontent, disenfranchisement, criminality, and—if left to fester too long—social unrest and sedition. The Los Angeles riots of 1992 and those taking place sporadically in other U.S. inner cities since that time—as well as the emergence of right-wing rural militia movements—are representative of a relatively restrained form of such societal conflict possibilities. Thus, the construct is meant to be non-partisan and seeks to only reflect that the new reality that we have found ourselves within is one in which "globalized capitalism is increasingly in variance with Western state-moderated capitalism which seeks to mitigate large inequalities in our social class structures."[184]

Twin Insurgency Effects

The next incremental shift in our understanding of class based insurgency potentials took place in 2015 with the publication of the twin insurgency construct by Nils Gilman—an editor of the earlier published work *Deviant Globalization*. This essay was written as a foreword for an international political economy book entitled *Global Criminal and Sovereign Free Economies and the Demise of the Western Democracies* edited by the authors of this work. The intent of Gilman's essay was to articulate the detrimental synergistic effects of the criminal and plutocratic insurgencies on the Western democracies. His essay remains the best coherent and integrative synopsis of the twin insurgency process and has been widely republished in online venues. It chronicles the failures of social modernism, characterizes plutocratic insurgency (the revolt of mainstream globalization's winners) and then criminal insurgency (the revolt of deviant globalization's winners), and then discusses the enclavization of microsovereignties and the end of the middle class.[185] He argues that:

> Seen from a spatial perspective, what both insurgencies represent is the replacement of the liberal ideal of uniform authority and rights within national spaces by *a kaleidoscopic array of de facto and de jure microsovereignties.* Rather than a single national space in which power is exercised and rights are enjoyed in a consistent and homogenous way by all residents, the cartography of the dual insurgency represents diverse enclaves of political authority and of social service provisioning arrangements…[186]

The synergistic effects of the twin insurgency—linked to the 'epochal compression' process later highlighted in the introduction to that international political economy book—focus on the gradual squeezing of the middle class from the plutocratic and criminal economic levels.[187] This results in some of this demographic achieving fortune while the majority is beginning to fall into the lower strata during which family debt levels begin to rise as those still economically 'hanging on by their fingernails' in the middle attempt to retain their present lifestyles. Additionally, the compression of the formal (i.e. legitimate) economy is taking place while taxable revenues are diminishing as more and more wealth and profit migrate out of governmental reach into the illicit and sovereign free economic levels.

As the plutocratic and criminal insurgencies increase in intensity, fewer instances of conventional warfare also break out. Lawyers and lobbyists from the top and armed and organized criminals from the bottom offer a challenge to states, further helping to undercut their monopoly on warmaking. Finally, sovereign rights are being eroded as areas of impunity emerge along with the inability of states to protect the integrity of their territorial borders in the face of human smuggling and mass migration, not only benefiting criminals but also plutocrats. The demise of sovereign rights also extends to new interpretations of international law and legal conventions. Rising public debt levels resulting in additional interest on debt servicing ultimately exacerbate these effects. Western governments thus have even less discretionary revenues for required public expenditures and, as a result, either have to make hard choices about where to allocate monies or are forced to engage in yearly cycles of new national debt accumulation. The latter is now evident in the U.S.— with the FY2019 budget deficit projected to be over $1 trillion that would be added to the present national public debt of over $21.5 trillion—following the 2017 H.R.1 - Tax Cuts and Jobs Act which, despite hopes for an egalitarian and working family friendly outcome, ultimately puts extra billions into the pockets of the plutocratic class at the expense of middle America.[188]

Autocratic Insurgency

One of the limitations of the twin (or dual) insurgency construct—within the context that it was initially articulated—is that it was singularly intended to articulate the epochal non-state threat 'compression process' directed at Western democracies. What it did not address was the relationship of plutocracy and criminality to 21st century (e.g. increasingly post-modern) autocratic states. More recent and evolving perceptions, since about June 2018, concerning the epochal change model vis-à-vis contemporary autocratic states—that is, states with concentrations of unrestrained policymakers (e.g. despotic rulers), repression of the governed, and bi-furcated upper and lower social class structures with an underdeveloped middle class—suggest that they are increasingly prospering from the modern to post-modern transition underway.[189] The relationship of autocratic states to internal, as well as global, inequality has been a positive and normative one. This orientation, when now combined with the more recent addition of authoritarian capitalism (as opposed to older communist planned central economic approach), has been highly beneficial to their form of social and political organization.

Additionally, autocratic states can be viewed, at least on one level, as a fusion of the worst elements of plutocratic and criminal interests.[190] Few realize that China and Russia have the world's two largest underground economies and draw strength from them in addition to their more formal economies that exist.[191] Autocracy thus represents an institutionalized pattern of plutocratic and criminal elite collusion that has gained legitimacy. Contemporary examples include the Russian Federation under Vladimir Putin (a former KGB officer) who has been in control since January 2000 and the People's Republic of China under Xi Jinping since November 2012. These autocratic states, in reality, are not too far removed along the continuum from kleptocratic, mafia, and criminal states such as North Korea, Venezuela, and Nigeria that are simply more blatant in their use of coercion and persecution against their citizens—as well as providing them even less basic services—and, as a result, suffer from higher levels of perceived illegitimacy. China's extrajudicial actions at Tiananmen Square in 1989, which may have resulted in at least 10,000 fatalities, and present policies of mass scale Uyghur 're-education camp' establishment and societal wide 'social credit-system' technology initiative directed at their citizenry suggest the true nature of such states.[192]

While authoritarian insurgency form thinking—with authoritarianism perceived as a plutocratic and criminal synthesis—is still relatively new, Seth Jones and Patrick Johnson theorized, as early as 2013, of the possibility of a Chinese insurgency form developing within the next decade. As they stated: "China could become increasingly involved in supporting insurgencies and counterinsurgencies if its economic and military power continues to increase and its global interest expands."[193] This potentiality was further discussed and analyzed in a March 2016 Strategic Studies Institute (SSI) paper with it being designated as an emergent Chinese authoritarianism insurgency form.[194] Indicators of this form developing are based on increasing Chinese initiatives such as China's Asian Infrastructure Investment Bank (AIIB), "Belt and Road" activities, significant political and economic investment inroads into both Africa and Latin America, man-made fortified island-reef construction to seize the South-China sea, and other activities which are coming into conflict with U.S. Pacific, and in fact global, interests. They are beginning to be met—at the very least from the Chinese perspective—with a U.S. containment initiative including new massive domestic trade sanctions being implemented by the current presidential administration.[195] A Chinese insurgency response that seeks to engage in strategic shaping operations to undermine the Western liberal-democratic order and instead promote authoritarian values that put a premium on social control, centralized decision making, and few individual freedoms now appears to represent a viable possibility. Such a response, when combined with ongoing Russian social media and election hacking activities focused domestically upon the U.S. to undermine its liberal-democratic values and consensus, add further credence that an authoritarian insurgency form beneficial to the position and privilege of elites in China, Russia, and their allies in other states (yet still very much haphazard and uncoordinated in its implementation) may now be manifesting itself.[196]

In summary, three commercially derived insurgency forms—and one synergistic fusion—derived from the 1993 Metz articulation and linked to differing social class structure orientations and the inherent inequalities existing as a result of them—are now posited to exist (See Table 3. and Figure 1.). The first, the criminal insurgency form represents the response of segments of the lower classes to being excluded from the formal economy. Some individuals, seeing no future for themselves or their children, have little choice but to engage in illicit economic pursuits while others were either born into the 'family business' or coerced into engaging in criminality. These individuals come together into organized groups to further their illicit economic activities and arm themselves for collective protective purposes against other similar armed and competing groups as well as governmental agents deployed in law enforcement, state security, and military units sent to curtail their activities, arrest them, and if need be kill them. The second, the plutocratic insurgency form represents the response of segments of the plutocratic (e.g. 1%-0.1%) classes who seek to remove themselves of the costs and burdens associated with the formal economy, and even citizenship, due the state—with tax avoidance utilizing lawyers and lobbyists being the principal means of preserving individual and family wealth and public goods being purchased solely as commodities (e.g. private education, private roads, and private security). Such plutocratic elements of our society increasingly seek extra-sovereign status and privilege at the expense of the majority of their less fortunate—and far less wealthy—American brethren.

INSURGENCY (& CAPITALISM) FORM	AUTHOR(S); DATE	SOCIAL CLASS INVOLVEMENT	END STATE & RATIONALE
Commercial (Warped Materialism; Illicit)	Metz; 1993	Lower Classes (Foreign Nationals)	Acquiring Material Possessions; Quasi-Political Distortion of Materialism
Criminal (Illicit; Deviant)	Sullivan; 2008	Lower Classes (Primarily Foreign Nationals)	Impunity of Action; *De Facto* Political Control; Illicit Wealth Generation
Plutocratic (Sovereign Free; Predatory)	Bunker; 2011	Upper Classes (U.S. & Foreign Nationals)	Winners of Globalization (Global Elites & Multinational Corporations) Removing Themselves from Sovereign Constraints; Maximizing Profits
Twin; Criminal (Illicit; Deviant) and Plutocratic (Sovereign Free; Predatory) Synergies	Gilman; 2015	Upper and Lower Classes (U.S. & Foreign Nationals)	Epochal 'Compression Process' Resulting in Liberal-Democratic State Form Deinstitutionalization; Synergistic Effects
Autocratic; Criminal and Plutocratic Fusion (Authoritarian)	Bunker and Sullivan; 2018 *(Chinese: Jones and Johnson; 2013)*	Upper Class (Primarily Foreign Nationals)	Authoritarian State (Post-Centrally Planned) Anti-Liberal-Democratic Environmental Shaping; Post-Modern State Form Challenger

**Table 3. Commercial Insurgency Forms
and Social Class Involvement**

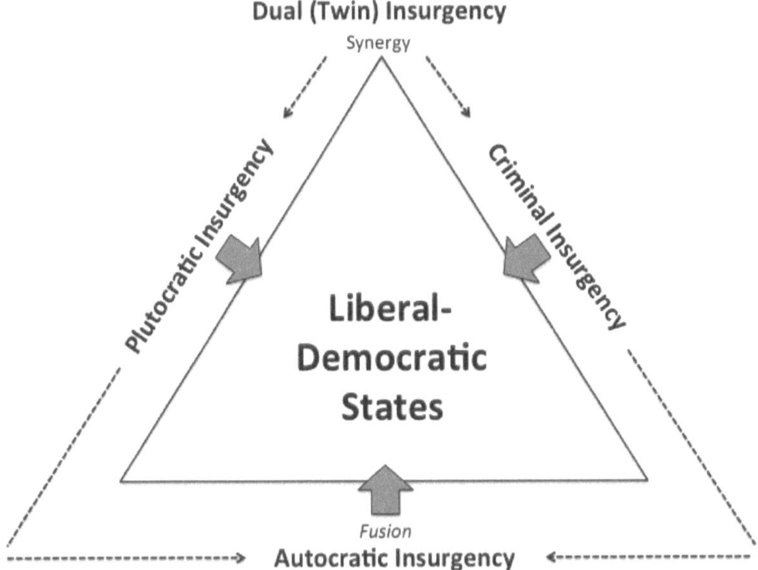

**Figure 1. Commercial Insurgency Forms
and Liberal-Democratic States**

As discussed above, together the first two insurgency forms are creating a synergy that is putting a vice-like compression on the Western democracies as part of the epochal transition process (Figure 2.). The third construct, autocratic insurgency, still in its emergent phase, is derived from two former centrally planned communist states—China and Russia—which have reconfigured themselves around authoritarian capitalism to maximize state power for their ruling elites vis-à-vis the new realities of a globalized and informational (e.g. 5th dimensional cyber) based world economy. It represents the autocratic state's attempts—not always successful—to become a relevant post-modern social and political organizational form contender.[197] Authoritarian insurgency thus undertakes strategic shaping operations aimed at the states of the world, and their citizens in order to induce environmental modification—conducive to authoritarian rather than liberal-democratic values—in their social, political, and economic institutions. While this insurgency form is presently viewed as only representing an external threat to the United States, the continuing increase of social inequality levels domestically, along with the further loss of societal consensus would result in our nation increasingly viewed as a 'house divided', and could conceivably become a domestic threat concern. Authoritarian insurgency could thus very well find allies within sectors of the plutocratic class within the U.S. This would represent a shift from liberal-democratic governance to one more authoritarian in orientation—a concern now increasingly expressed by large numbers of U.S. citizens. This could create a reversion back to Gilded Age politics and class relations—at a minimum—with the now very real potential for the loss of over a century of progressive social democratic and civil rights programs and initiatives.

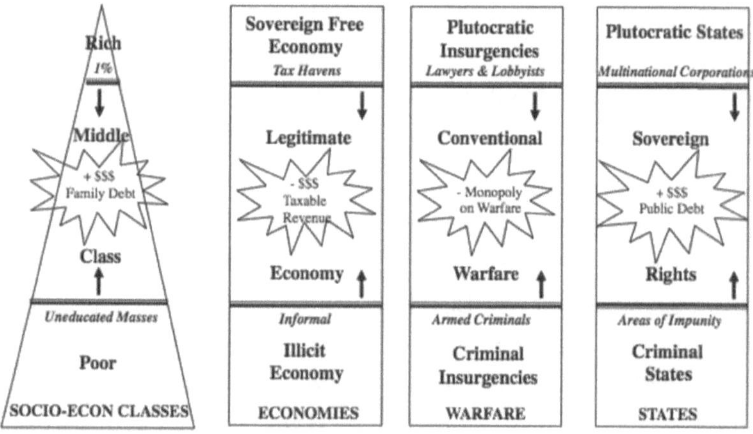

Figure 2. Compression Effect on the Western Democracies[198]

VI

Armed Forces Implications and Governmental Policy Response

At the most basic level, the armed forces—as a microcosm of U.S. society—are being plagued by various stressors including the risk of personnel potentially embracing tribal and extremist allegiances (such as gang, radical Islamist, and white nationalism), being asked to engage in morally ambiguous 'gray area' missions with no clear cut allies and enemies, and being deployed in endless campaigns by elected officials and civilian elites most of whom (80% in 2015) have never served in the military. Furthermore, the services are no longer serving as a melting pot for society—with fewer in poorer communities, largely minorities (due to the lack of quality secondary education making it harder to pass increasingly stringent skills tests) as well as fewer elites (who can make more money in the private sector) serving. Moreover, the shift towards a 'capital-intensive' force structure has caused their budgetary expenditures to become a focus for both politician and public attention in times of increasing governmental budget constraints.

These concerns are ultimately linked to the deeper ones related to the changing nature of capitalism, due to globalization and advanced informational technologies, and concurrent levels of rising inequality. The latter are being expressed worldwide, in the West, and most importantly in the United States itself and will have implications related to the commercial insurgency form variants emerging, the war over social and political organization taking place (as a component of the transition from the modern to post-modern epochal transition underway), and concerns for developing state and environmental integrity. These armed forces implications and the suggested governmental policy responses related to them are as follows:

Commercial Insurgency Forms

New insurgency forms are difficult for the U.S. Army and Department of Defense in general to accede to due to the fact that they exist 'out of paradigm' within their institutional perceptions of 'what is' and 'what is not' a national security threat vis-a-vis their traditional roles and missions responsibilities. During the Cold War, the U.S. military focused upon Maoist insurgency type threats (i.e. Communist revolutionary derived) that had an inherent political component to them. During the initial post-Cold War era and into the present day, the earlier insurgency form was superseded by the radical Islamist insurgency form, derived initially from Shia (e.g. Hezbollah) and later Sunni (e.g. al Qaeda and later the Islamic State) based spirituality. Radical Islamist insurgency represents a fusion of extreme elements of religious and political components promoted primarily by non-state actors. These actors promote Islamic based societies rejecting Western Reformation and Enlightenment based ideology. It required a horrific experience derived from the 9/11 attack (i.e. mass American citizenry blood on the pavement) for U.S. governmental authority to recognize that such a new insurgency form had indeed emerged and represented a direct military threat to U.S. domestic as well as global interests.

We are now in the process of a second new insurgency form actively maturing—one broadly defined as commercial insurgency. This new type of insurgency is even more alien to our modern institutional perceptions than the radical Islamist form because— in its initial criminal and plutocratic manifestations—it is devoid of any form of pre-meditated political (Clausewitzian) component. With its basis drawn from the accumulation of monetary wealth and resources—and the required impunity to engage in such pursuits by compromising and/or bypassing sovereign state laws, courts, and extractive (e.g. income tax) institutions—it presently functions outside of existing American military roles and missions except under the most egregious conditions when *de facto* criminal state emergence begins to result.[199] Additionally, given that this insurgency form represents a component of globalized capitalism, that is both predatory and hyper-rational in its profit seeking focus, it can be viewed as the antithesis of the older state-moderated form of capitalism that liberal-democratic states once flourished within. In a sense, the global techno-economic environment of the early 21st century—if not before—is turning 'toxic' to the Western states and their peoples who politically organized around notions of mass political enfranchisement, individual liberties, economic equality, and middle class industrial age derived social class structures.

A second revelation, in addition to the fact that the new variant of global capitalism that has emerged represents an increasing threat to U.S. middle class interests, is that China and to some extent Russia—both former Communist states based upon centrally planned economies—have reconfigured themselves into authoritarian regimes seeking to flourish in the new realities and potentials the techno-economic environment of globalization offers. These regimes have no ethical qualms—China, for instance, has been described as having a 'techno-utilitarianism' philosophy[200]—about engaging in predatory and optimizing strategies that leverage the illicit economy as an additional economic extractive base. These increasingly post-modern configured states, representative of fusions of criminality and plutocracy, have the very real potential of engaging in their own forms of autocratic insurgency as a direct challenge to the global influence and interests of the U.S. and her Western allies. We have already witnessed the opening shots in such a potential conflict with the use of fake news and divisive social media by the Russian state and ongoing hacking campaigns by both Russia and China directed at the U.S.[201]

Given the oblique and very alien nature of commercial insurgency based threats (via its criminal, plutocratic, and authoritarian manifestations), no immediate, near, or even medium term 'trigger event' remotely approximating a 9/11 type experience for the American government or its public is expected to take place. Therefore, this new insurgency form will continue to be discounted and ignored by the U.S. Department of Defense and, until a lot of American blood is spilled by an entity engaging in this form of insurgency, such a prognosis will continue to hold. The U.S. thus exists in a 'frog in the pot' reality where economic and social class conditions are changing a degree at a time as the pot begins to heat up but the shift is so subtle that little realization exists that anything is amiss—at least from the perspective that it is the 'invisible hand' of unfettered global capitalism that actually lit the fire and is actively stirring the pot.

Thus, as it presently stands (See Table 4.), criminal insurgency has low to moderate implications for armed forces response requirements and may result in either U.S. law enforcement (typically) or U.S. military mission leads supporting our allies primarily situated in Latin America. Preferably, all-of-government task forces are utilized. Of immediate concern are street and prison gangs found in Central America—specifically 18th Street and Mara Salvatrucha (MS-13)—and the Mexican cartels with the Cártel de Sinaloa (CDS; Sinaloa Cartel) and Cártel de Jalisco Nueva Generación (CJNG; Jalisco New Generation Cartel) being of most significance. The plutocratic insurgency form, on the other hand, is devoid of a present military mandate to respond against it—unless of course mercenary forces (something akin to the Russian Wagner group for instance) were in the employ of a transnational plutocratic entity and directly threatened U.S. interests. The ongoing expectation is that varying U.S. governmental agencies with either a legal or economic focus would be investigating such extra-sovereign entities for their nefarious and tax-dodging activities supported by federal law enforcement for arrest and prosecution purposes. In the case of the autocratic insurgency form—which would have a political basis related to promoting reconfigured Russian and/or Chinese governmental interests linked to their predatory capitalism and U.S. influence denial pursuits—we have not as of yet seen the emergence of such a commercial insurgency variant. U.S. military response would be that of intelligence community monitoring and analysis to provide early warning of such activities combined with U.S. State and Department of Defense behavioral and environmental shaping operations to limit the emergence of such a form and its subsequent impact. If it did indeed arise, though, implementation barriers to this form are viewed as existing which may limit its eventual emergence and overall effectiveness.

ARMED FORCES (& U.S. GOV) IMPLICATIONS	POLICY RESPONSE
Criminal Insurgency -Contemporary -Low to Moderate Implications	*Some Military Missions* *Federal Law Enforcement and/or Military Lead* -All-of-Government
Plutocratic Insurgency -Contemporary -No Present Implications	*No Military Mandate* *Varying Governmental Agencies* -Legal and Economic Focus -Federal Law Enforcement
Authoritarian Insurgency -Potential; Near to Midterm Significant Implication Potentials -Implementation Barriers Exist	*No Present Military Missions* *Intelligence Community* -Monitoring & Analysis *State & DoD* -Behavioral and Environmental Shaping

**Table 4. Commercial Insurgency Forms:
Implications and Policy Response**[202]

These limited law enforcement and 'counter-insurgency' military responses to the commercial insurgency form variants will continue to be overshadowed by our ongoing global conflict with radical Islamist insurgents. At some point in the future, however, either at the U.S. Army War College or new Army Futures Command level, some consideration should be given to additional study, analysis, and potential wargaming of commercial insurgency form manifestations. It would be preferable to pro-actively position the U.S. Army for its future response to this new and emerging insurgency form rather than to reactively respond to it due to a day after blood on the pavement 'trigger event,' which likely still exists somewhere far over the time horizon.[203]

War Over Social and Political Organization

The changing nature of global capitalism, the fielding of advanced technologies, and rising inequality levels will transcend the level of new and emergent insurgency forms and also have direct implications on state force structure, governance, and social class structure futures. These implications will exist within the epochal context of 'war over social and political organization' (how people will live, organize, and the values that they will share in the future) as opposed to more traditionalist (and modernist) Clausewitizian imperatives related to the preservation and extension of state prerogatives and sovereignty. New warmaking entities will arise during this era from subnational groupings (e.g. the global al Qaeda and Islamic States networks and gang and cartel organizations in Latin America) as well as supra-national entities forming (e.g. the European Union) in addition to traditional states that will all be engaging in this global conflict over what the organizational form successor to the Westphalian state will be.[204]

The Army is at the forefront of U.S. efforts to field a future force that will be engaging in mid-21st century warfare as a component of this ongoing conflict. This future force—which will leverage the Department of Defense's Third Offset Strategy emphasizing deep-learning systems (e.g. AI), human-machine collaboration, human-machine combat teaming, assisted human operations, and network-enabled, cyber-hardened weapons[205]—will be fundamentally different than legacy based armored ground forces though will still likely be utilizing some of its major platforms such as the M1 Abrams series main battle tank. From earlier sections of this monograph, it is clear that restraints on the future force will center upon increasing U.S. governmental shortfalls and rising debt servicing—the Army will be existing in another age of austerity and will be asked to once again do more with less resources.[206] Additionally, the recruitment pool for the Army is shrinking with the decline of the middle class. The elites within American society are simply uninterested in military service or careers while at the same time those from the growing lower classes are increasingly unfit for military service due to low test scores, lack of education, medical and narcotics use issues, and criminal records. This has resulted in the phenomena of 'increased regional and familial concentration within the armed forces' from the remaining components of the middle class.[207] This has further served to decouple military service from the mass of the American public and created a 'warrior caste' mentality based on multigenerational military families whose 'family business' is that of fighting for the state.[208] This trend would be somewhat less troubling if it were not for the fact that private security and mercenary forces (i.e. armed contractors) were returning to the battlefield once again in mass as a byproduct of the post-modern transition underway.

Gained from the above policy perspective, three policy responses are suggested for the U.S. Army related to the future force (See Table 5.). First, given fiscal and personnel constraints as well as advances in robotics and artificial intelligence, a smaller (from a human personnel perspective) and more lethal force is advocated for general warfighting purposes. It would include the fielding of armed robotic systems with human only, human-machine, and machine only force packages being developed as part of the experimental force.[209] Second, the shift from an industrial to an informational based Army organization needs to fully take place. To date, Army informational adaptations can at best be considered a 'bolt on' effort to its industrial based organizational schema. This change will ultimately require the full transition from a hierarchical to networked command and control (C²) structure for optimization purposes. This will be extremely disruptive for Army culture as it would require a reconfiguration of the present rank structure based on bureaucratic 'line and block' management principals into something far more flatter and entrepreneurial. Third, a mission reorientation of the Army National Guard—remaining primarily a human based force—is advocated with a primary focus upon internal stability and support with less-lethal/riot control and military police functionality. The reason for this change is to allow the Army additional state (SAD; State Active Duty & Title 32) and national (Title 10) level capacity for domestic and foreign crisis response missions. Such a mission reorientation is prudent given the likelihood of future domestic societal unrest derived from increasing levels of inequality—and unemployment potentials—as well as ongoing foreign state fragility and failure, environmental degradation, and mass migration and population dislocation. Based on this force structure schema, the Army reserve could be positioned as either a legacy armor and mechanized force (human only), a ready reserve human-machine and machine force, a stability and support oriented force (for foreign deployment only), or a blending of all three capability sets.

ARMED FORCES (& U.S. GOV) IMPLICATIONS	POLICY RESPONSE

The Future Force
  -Budget Shortfalls and Rising Debt Servicing
  -Polarized Recruitment Pools
  -Robotics and Artificial Intelligence
  -Private Security (Mercenary) Issue
	Create a Smaller and More Lethal Force
	  -Less Personnel
	  -Field Armed Robotic Systems (Droids & Drones)
	Shift from Industrial to Informational
	  -Hierarchical to Networked
	  -Bureaucratic to Entrepreneurial
	New Army National Guard Mission
	  -Refocus on Internal Stability & Support
	  -Less-Lethal/Riot Control & Military Police

Future Governance (State-Form)
  -Loss of Domestic Political Consensus
  -Shift Towards Domestic Authoritarian Tendencies
	Remain Apolitical
	  -Status Quo
	  -Watch from the Sidelines
	Become Politicized
	  -Hazardous to civil-military relations and civilian oversight

Future Social Class Structure (& Social Cohesion)
  -Middle Class Compression
  -Rising Inequality (Rich & Poor)
  -Rising Unemployment
	Take No Action
	Provide National Service Opportunities
	  -1-2 Year Employment (Teach Job Skills)
	Income Redistribution [Broader Governmental]
	  -Universal Basic Income (UBI)
	  -Guaranteed Minimum Income (GMI)

Table 5. War Over Social and Political Organization: Implications and Policy Response

The next implication is at the U.S. governmental level and focuses upon what future governance will look like in our country (including the possible state-form itself). It goes without saying that domestic political consensus has been lost with great levels of polarization taking place between the Republican and Democratic parties along with a vast centrist grouping of our citizens having opted out into an independent, yet politically impotent, third party. At the same time—and as a direct result of losing political moderation vis-à-vis the rise of right and left wing extremist politics—we have seen the rise of populism and authoritarian tendencies being promoted in narratives and policies even within the government itself. Political strategies including promoting calculated divisiveness between the right and the left and an ongoing and almost daily spectacle of mini-crisis has only served to further open up divisions in our society rather than mitigate them. Still, the right and left debate focusing increasingly on the differing value systems and world views held by traditional rural based America and more liberal urban America is, however, only a symptom of the underlying issue of growing wealth inequality, a deficit of full time living wage employment opportunities, and lack of public monies earmarked to be spent on governmental goods and services within our society. Such societal stressors have resulted in segments of American citizenry at times acting like participants in a 1960s mouse utopia experiment gone bad, with fierce backbiting over scarce resources and deviant behaviors (e.g. weekly active shooter events) becoming more pronounced.[210] As class polarization becomes increasingly apparent, and the upper classes continue to effectively privatize and commoditize governmental goods and services, this is the debate that should be focused upon.

From a U.S. Army perspective—the status quo approach in which its corporate body and personnel are both to remain non-politicized and apolitical servants of higher level elected governmental authority is the one the Army and its personnel are by law and statue required to follow. Despite any perceived *de facto* backing of the elite, for the Army and/or its personnel to become politicized would be a very dangerous proposition for civil-military relations and effective civilian oversight.[211] This leaves our Army politically sidelined—at least into the foreseeable future—over engaging in the debate about what future U.S. governance may look like and to what extent rising authoritarianism from within may challenge our liberal-democratic traditions.

Closely tied to the above implications are those related to our future social class structure and the dynamics related to the social cohesion within our society. It is an undisputed fact that our nation is actively feeling the adverse effects of middle class compression and rising inequality between the rich and the poor. While the employment market—at least on the surface due to historically low unemployment levels—appears robust, this is a misnomer. Secure full time jobs with benefits and retirement packages are becoming increasingly scare and less and less of our population is adequately trained and educated for more intellectually demanding cognitive labor based work. Additionally, while hope has existed that off-shored jobs would return to our country, when corporations do come home the jobs are typically no-shored—that is to say, replaced by deep-learning (AI) systems and robotics. In fact, the expectation is that the rich will continue to get richer and the poor will continue to get poorer in American society with such AI systems technically being able to endanger as much as 40-50% of both cognitive and physical labor based employment domestically over the next ten to twenty years.[212]

From a related policy perspective, one governmental response could be for the U.S. Army to maintain its current programs and recruitment while our socio-economic structures shift and our internal social cohesion continues to gradually erode. It would thus remain economically neutral as a corollary to its ongoing apolitical position. The other option is for the government to institute a governmental national service type program under the auspices of the Army that would provide

1-2 years of employment and job skills for the less skilled underclasses. By default, this is often what basic enlistment already has provided for many of those citizens who take the oath of service. They just currently serve for a longer period of time. By cutting enlistment time for these individuals, the Army experience could also provide its previous moderating functions to a wider range of individuals within society.

The other broader governmental response to growing levels of inequality and unemployment potentials in our society is more radical in its approach. It would recognize that some sort of income redistribution program will likely be required for future social cohesion purposes. Such governmental welfare payments would have to move beyond the stigma of 'food stamp' approaches. This may initially be near impossible to sell to a nation still following narratives of rugged individualism, individual and family self-reliance, and the Horatio Alger mythos that anyone can prosper in our capitalist society as long as the work hard and persevere in their profession. Over time, however, if and when domestic strife broke out, the palatability of this approach would increase, especially if the levels of societal unrest became heightened. This program would be derived from either universal basic income (UBI) or guaranteed minimum income (GMI) approaches with quite a body of policy literature already existing related to it.[213] Rather than a 'free ride' taking place for those accepting such governmental support, however, it would be tied to job retraining and/or societal cohesion-enhancing (humanistic) types of employment as proposed by Kai-Fu Lee—former president of Google China.[214] One caveat is that job retraining to get many of our citizens off of such a 'government payment system' may at some point become impossible if the projections related to the coming wave of AI and robotics based economic production are indeed accurate.

Developing State and Environmental Integrity

The implications stemming from this manuscript related to developing state and environmental integrity concerns focus on rising inequality levels vis-à-vis the continuing viability of such states, the degradation of their water and food resources, and the ensuing mass migration and dislocation of their populations that this may entail. Fragile and failed states have very limited capacity to deliver public goods and services to their citizens or contend with man-made or environmental crises. The perception that the structural constitution of the majority of the world's states is not getting better—due to both internal and external factors such as ongoing corruption, disaster (predatory) capitalism, growing multinational corporate power, increasing overpopulation, crumbling infrastructure, spreading sectarianism (and tribalism), and religious extremism—is in line with the writings of Homer-Dixon, Kaplan, Hertz, Davis, Klein, and others.[215] Additionally, current trends in global warming are beginning to wreck the ecosystems of numerous states due to fresh water shortages for some of them (including India, Iran, Jordan, and South Africa) and rising sea water levels for others (including Indonesia, Thailand, Myanmar, and Bangladesh). Even the challenge posed by natural wildfires has been drastically altered. For strong state capacity regions—such as California, that is now suffering its worst wildfires in history—this challenge is substantial; for fragile states such natural disasters have become almost insurmountable.[216] This is all taking place while the mass of humanity is increasing moving to the megacities and the teeming slums that surround them primarily situated in the world's underdeveloped regions. Those who are devoid of economic resources living in such weak political capacity states either face violence, starvation, or other forms of peril if they remain in place during times of crisis or readily become refugees as they flee from such Hobbesian and life threatening circumstances.

Based on the above perceptions, global crises are expected to remain steady state if not actively increase, as is currently the projection. This means that our government will be constantly called upon to provide aid to weak capacity states and the relatively impoverished citizens—the bulk of their populations—that are affected by them.[217] This will have direct implications on broader U.S. governmental and Army policy response that can be viewed primarily in four ways (See Table 6.). The initial component of this is that some form of ongoing and wide-ranging governmental geo-political analysis will be required rather than action being media attention cycle driven. Such a process will need to utilize a metric based upon national interest, physical proximity to the U.S. and her allies, and the opportunity cost (and likely competitor gain) involved in making a decision to provide material support. Given what is expected to be increasingly constrained U.S. economic resources, a political triage approach that focuses on a cost-benefit and resource conservation strategy should be implemented as a component of this approach. The reality is the U.S. cannot disengage from its global responsibilities—and the alliance network that it has created to promote a liberal-democratic order—but, at the same time, cannot sustain (from a budgetary perspective) its present level of military deployments and associated activities. Disengagement would result in the creation of 'influence voids' left by the U.S. being filled by China or Russia—or, even in some instances, al Qaeda, the Islamic State, and various organized criminal entities. Given this sobering reality, the only pragmatic course of action is for the U.S. to initiate a better burden sharing global security arrangement with its liberal-democratic allies (and even its client authoritarian regimes). This would entail the GDP indexed contributions of those allies to the collective global defense be increased while the U.S. share is decreased at a commensurate and agreed upon level. From an Army (and Joint Force) response capabilities level, this ties back to the need for both a precision engagement capacity (derived from an increasingly AI and armed robotic derived force) as well as stability and support—riot control, and military police—capabilities that can allow for the provision of direct support to both U.S. allies and developing states when the criteria is met for such aid to be provided.

ARMED FORCES (& U.S. GOV) IMPLICATIONS	POLICY RESPONSE

Developing State and Environmental Integrity
    -Fragile and Failed States
    -Environmental Degradation—Water & Food
    -Mass Migration and Dislocated Populations
	Geo-Political Analysis [Broader Governmental]
	        -National Interest
	        -Physical Proximity to the U.S./Allies
	        -Opportunity Cost/Competitor Gain
	Triage Approach [Broader Governmental]
	        -Cost-Benefit
	        -Resource Conservation
	Defense Burden Sharing
	        -With Liberal-Democratic Allies
	        -Commensurate Level Increases/U.S. Decrease
	Response Capabilities
	        -Precision Engagement
	        -Stability and Support
	        -Riot Control and Military Police

Table 6. Developing State and Environmental Integrity: Implications and Policy Response

As a closing policy observation, individual states and societies have historically upon more than a number of occasions become polarized with large economic disparities resulting. At some point, this is akin to a very large and ongoing game of Monopoly™. The new players entering are either lucky enough to take over the positions of a few of its winners or are forced—along with the majority—to take on the role of predetermined losers that must navigate the board devoid of any form of tangible wealth or resources. Instances of such extreme societal levels of inequality include Athens during the period of Solon reforms in the 6th century BC, France just prior to its revolution in 1789, and Russia leading up to its revolution of 1917. Some form of more equitable economic redistribution is typically achieved within these societies only as a result of some sort of catastrophic event—war, revolution, state collapse, or even plague.[218] Using the same writ-large and ongoing Monopoly™ game analogy, the playing board is literally overturned with a new and more equitable restart of the game for the players—representative of the citizens of the body politic—begun all over again.

Fortunately, in the United States, we have seen the violent (and semi-violent) outcomes of similarly high levels of inequality and political disenfranchisement (given that governance is about the allocation of societal goods and resources) manifest themselves only sporadically. While the Los Angeles riots of August 1965 and April-May 1992 have increasingly faded into distant memory, they are indicative of what happens when the polarization of the rich and the poor, class and privilege, and hope and despair takes place with those—in these instances, primarily ethnic minorities—getting a 'raw deal' from the dominant political system lashing out in anger. More recently, the Occupy Wall Street (OWS) movement spanning September 2011 through May 2012 saw the 99%—primarily composed of younger white citizens—protest against rising inequality and the growing economic dominance of the 1%. Such mass protests have long since ended due in part to the ongoing post-recession recovery of the economy. Still, they are indicative, along with the earlier Los Angeles riots, of the underlying potentials for significant social unrest, now likely cutting across ethnic lines, if societal inequality, the compression of the middle class, lack of employment opportunities, and political disenfranchisement of the lower classes (which appear to be growing in size) should continue to increase. As a nation, we should proactively position ourselves so that the conditions leading to such high levels of social unrest do not manifest themselves. This may be extremely difficult, however, as rising levels of inequality are not only a U.S. specific issue but are also globally systemic in nature as a component of the epochal transition taking place. Still, this course of action is much more preferable than either seeing our nation incrementally become more authoritarian in nature (i.e. police state-like, actively engaging in social control, and corrupt) or suffer a domestic or international catastrophe that serves to ultimately restore an equitable balance between the haves (the economic winners) and have nots (the economic losers) in our society.[219]

End Notes

1   Although it is recognized that the perceived causes, nature, and inevitability of that inequality is certainly not without dissent.

2   For a more detailed explanation of this and related measures of income inequality, see S. Jenkins and P. Van Kerm, Chapter 3, The Measurement of Economic Inequality, *The Oxford Handbook of Economic Inequality*, 2009: 40-67.

3   Anthony B. Atkinson, *Inequality: What Can Be Done?* Cambridge, MA, 2015: 16-17.

4   Thomas Piketty, *The Economics of Inequality*. Arthur Goldhammer, Trans. Cambridge, MA: Belknap Press: 2015, 10.

5   See B. Nolan and I. Marx, Ch. 13 "Economic Inequality, Poverty, and Social Exclusion," *The Oxford Handbook of Economic Inequality*, 2009: 316-317.

6   See, for example, the middle class income range table using data from the 2017 U.S. Census in Kimberly Amadeo, "Middle Class Income: Are You in the Middle Class." *The Balance*. July 19, 2018, https://www.thebalance.com/definition-of-middle-class-income-4126870.

7   Pew Research Center, "The American middle class is stable in size, but losing ground financially to upper-income families." 6 September 2018: 5, http://www.pewresearch.org/fact-tank/2018/09/06/the-american-middle-class-is-stable-in-size-but-losing-ground-financially-to-upper-income-families/.

8   Richard Reeves et. al., *Defining the middle class: Cash, credentials, or culture?* Brookings Institution Report. 7 May 2018, https://www.brookings.edu/research/defining-the-middle-class-cash-credentials-or-culture/.

9   Sam Drabble et. al., "The Rise of a Global Middle Class: Global societal trends to 2030." Thematic report 6. RAND Europe. 2015: 11, https://www.rand.org/pubs/research_reports/RR920z6.html.

10 Rakesh Kochhar, "How Americans compare with the global middle class." Pew Research Center. 9 July 2015, http://www.pewresearch.org/fact-tank/2015/07/09/how-americans-compare-with-the-global-middle-class/.

11 Mario Pezzini, "An emerging middle class." *OECD Observer.* 2011, http://oecdobserver.org/news/fullstory.php/aid/3681/An_emerging_middle_class.html.

12 *World Migration Report 2018.* Geneva: International Organization for Migration (IOM). 28 November 2017: 40-43, https://www.iom.int/wmr/world-migration-report-2018.

13 Miguel Nino-Zarazua et. al., "Income Inequality in a Globalising World," VOX CEPR Policy Portal, 20 September 2016: 2, https://voxeu.org/article/income-inequality-globalising-world.

14 Tara Copp, "President Trump orders 5,200 active duty troops to the US-Mexico Border." *Military Times.* 29 October 2018, https://www.militarytimes.com/news/your-military/2018/10/29/trump-orders-5200-active-duty-troops-to-us-mexico-border/.

15 Branko Milanovic, *Global Inequality.* Cambridge, MA: The Belknap Press, 2016: 14-15.

16 The decimal rather than the percent Gini will be used throughout for comparison purposes although one may been used over the other in the original text.

17 World Bank Group, *Poverty and Shared Prosperity 2016: Taking on Inequality.* 2016: 9, https://openknowledge.worldbank.org/handle/10986/25078.

18 Miguel Nino-Zarazua et. al., "Income Inequality in a Globalising World,": 2-3.

19 Miguel Nino-Zarazua et. al., "Global Inequality: Relatively Lower, Absolutely Higher." *The Review of Income and Wealth.* Series 63, No. 4, December 2017: 664-665.

20 Ibid: 681.

21 William Robinson, *Global Capitalism Theory and the Emergence of Transnational Elites.* Helsinki: United Nations University, UNU-WIDER Working Paper No. 2010/02, January 2010: 1-2, https://www.wider.unu.edu/publication/global-capitalism-theory-and-emergence-transnational-elites.

22 Ibid: 11.

23 This chart first appeared in World Bank Policy Research Working Paper 6719 *Global Income Distribution: From the Fall of the Berlin Wall to the Great Recession*, December 2013: 42, https://openknowledge. worldbank.org/handle/10986/16935. The authors, Christopher Lakner and Branko Milonovic, referred to it therein as "Figure 6. Quasi-non-anonymous growth incidence curve." For a good graphic comparison of the 'elephant chart' and its variants, see Justin Sandefur, "Chart of the Week #1: Is the Elephant Graph Flattening Out?" Center for Global Development, 4 January 2018, https://www.cgdev.org/blog/ chart-week-1-elephant-graph-flattening-out.

24 Branko Milanovic, *Global Inequality*: 18-22.

25 Ibid: 24-26.

26 See, for example: Adam Corlett, *Examining an Elephant*. Resolution Foundation Report, 2016, https://www.resolutionfoundation.org/ app/uploads/2016/09/Examining-an-elephant.pdf; Caroline Freund, "Deconstructing Branko Milanovic's "Elephant Chart": Does It Show What Everyone Thinks?" Realtime Economic Issues Watch, Peterson Institute for International Economics (PIIE). 30 November 2016, https://piie.com/blogs/realtime-economic-issues-watch/ deconstructing-branko-milanovics-elephant-chart-does-it-show; and Homi Kharas and Brina Seidel, *What's happening to the world income distribution? The elephant chart revisited*. Washington, DC: Brookings Report, April 2018, https://www.brookings.edu/research/ whats-happening-to-the-world-income-distribution-the-elephant-chart-revisited/.

27 *World Inequality Report 2018*: 13.

28 Ibid: 9-11, 17.

29 Homi Kharas, *The Unprecedented Expansion of the Global Middle Class*, Global Economy & Development Working Paper 100. Washington, DC: Brookings, February 2017: 2, 19, https://www.brookings.edu/wp-content/uploads/2017/02/global_20170228_global-middle-class.pdf.

30 Heather Long and Leslie Shapiro, "Does $60,000 make you middle class or wealthy on Planet Earth." *The Washington Post*. 20 August 2018, https://www.washingtonpost.com/business/2018/08/20/ does-make-you-middle-class-or-wealthy-planet-earth/?utm_ term=.7272681238a1.

31 Oxfam, *Reward Work, Not Wealth*. Nairobi: January 2018: 10, https:// www.oxfam.org/en/research/reward-work-not-wealth.

32 Jason Hickel, "Global inequality may be much worse than we think." *The Guardian*. 8 April 2016, https://www.theguardian.com/global-development-professionals-network/2016/apr/08/global-inequality-may-be-much-worse-than-we-think.

33 Oxfam, *Reward Work, Not Wealth*: 12.

34 For one such commentary, see Jennifer Blanke, "Is technological change creating a new global economy?" World Economic Forum. 19 January 2016, https://www.weforum.org/agenda/2016/01/is-technological-change-creating-a-new-global-economy/. For the study it is based upon, see Carl Frey and Michael Osborne, *The Future of Employment*. Oxford: Oxford Martin Programme on Technology and Employment, 17 September 2013, https://www.oxfordmartin.ox.ac.uk/downloads/academic/The_Future_of_Employment.pdf.

35 Susan Lund and Laura Tyson, "Globalization is Not in Retreat: Digital Technology and the Future of Trade." *Foreign Affairs*. May/June 2018: 2-3, 11.

36 Zia Qureshi, "Globalization, technology, and inequality: It's the policies, stupid." *Brookings Blog*. 16 February 2018, https://www.brookings.edu/blog/up-front/2018/02/16/globalization-technology-and-inequality-its-the-policies-stupid/.

37 *World Inequality Report 2018*: 9.

38 Jeffrey D. Sachs, "The Strategic Significance of Global Inequality." *The Washington Quarterly*. Vol. 24. Iss. 3, 2001: 187-198.

39 Oxfam, *Reward Work, Not Wealth*: 8.

40 Erik Sherman, "America is the Richest, and Most Unequal Country." *Fortune*. 30 September 2015, http://fortune.com/2015/09/30/america-wealth-inequality/.

41 Adam Corlett, *Examining an Elephant*, Resolution Foundation Report, 2016, p. 25.

42 Organization for Economic Cooperation and Development (OECD) website, https://data.oecd.org [Accessed 6 November 2018].

43 Zsolt Darvas, "EU income inequality decline: Views from an income shares perspective." *Breugels Blog*. 5 July 2018, http://bruegel.org/2018/07/eu-income-inequality-decline-views-from-an-income-shares-perspective/.

44 Mark Abadi, "Income Inequality is Growing Across the US—Here's How Bad It Is In Every State." *Money Magazine*. 21 March 2018, http://time.com/money/5207987/income-inequality-every-state/.

45 Francesco Grigoli, "A New Twist in the Link Between Inequality and

Economic Development." *International Monetary Fund (IMF) Blog*. 11 May 2017, https://blogs.imf.org/2017/05/11/a-new-twist-in-the-link-between-inequality-and-economic-development/.

46 Congressional Budget Office (CBO), *The Distribution of Household Income 2014*. Washington, DC: 19 March 2018: 3, https://www.cbo.gov/publication/53597.

47 Emily Stewart, "One chart that shows how much worse income inequality is in America than Europe." *VOX*. 29 July 2018, https://www.vox.com/2018/7/29/17627134/income-inequality-chart.

48 Corlett, *Examining an Elephant*: 26.

49 *World Inequality Report 2018*: 89.

50 William Gale et. al., *Winners and Losers After Paying for the Tax Cuts and Jobs Act*. Washington, DC: Tax Policy Center. 8 December 2017: 21, https://www.taxpolicycenter.org/publications/winners-and-losers-after-paying-tax-cuts-and-jobs-act/full.

51 Jen Deaderick, "The Housing Market Crash and Wealth Inequality in the U.S." *The National Bureau of Economic Research (NBER) Digest*. January 2018, https://www.nber.org/digest/jan18/w24085.shtml.

52 Erik Sherman, "America is the Richest, and Most Unequal, Country." *Fortune*. 30 September 2015, http://fortune.com/2015/09/30/america-wealth-inequality/.

53 Allianz Financial Services, *Global Wealth Report 2018*. Munich: Alliance SE, 26 September 2018: 63, 68-69, https://www.allianz.com/en_GB/economic_research/publications/specials_fmo/agwr18e.html.

54 Will Martin, "The 1% are getting richer and its not going to stop any time soon." *The Independent UK*. 10 April 2018, https://www.independent.co.uk/money/worlds-richest-are-getting-even-richer-global-wealth-a8297421.html.

55 Michael Hiltzik, "The truth about income inequality, in six amazing charts," *Los Angeles Times*. 7 August 2018, http://www.latimes.com/business/hiltzik/la-fi-hiltzik-inequality-20180807-story.html.

56 *World Inequality Report 2018*: 205.

57 Sophia Hardach, "The State of the US Economy in 11 charts," World Economic Forum. 2 July 2018: 5-6, https://www.weforum.org/agenda/2018/07/heres-the-state-of-the-us-economy-in-11-charts/.

58 Kari Paul, "America's 1% hasn't controlled this much wealth since before the Great Depression." *MarketWatch*. 5 August 2018, https://www.marketwatch.com/story/wealth-inequality-in-the-us-is-almost-as-bad-as-it-was-right-before-the-great-depression-2018-07-19.

59 Jim Wang, "Here's the average net worth of Americans at every age." *Business Insider.* 5 June 2017, https://www.businessinsider.com/heres-the-average-net-worth-of-americans-at-every-age-2017-6?r=UK&IR=T.

60 Board of Governors of the Federal Reserve, *Report on the Economic Well-Being of U.S. Households in 2017.* May 2018, https://www.federalreserve.gov/publications/files/2017-report-economic-well-being-us-households-201805.pdf.

61 Eleanor Rose, "Seventy percent of British workers are 'chronically broke or only just able to get by." *Evening Standard.* 25 January 2018, https://www.standard.co.uk/news/uk/seventy-per-cent-of-british-workers-are-chronically-broke-research-reveals-a3749701.html.

62 OECD, *United States Economic forecast summary.* Washington, DC: May 2018, http://www.oecd.org/unitedstates/united-states-economic-forecast-summary.htm.

63 U.S. Bureau of the Census, *Real Median Household Income in the United States* [MEHOINUSA672N]. Federal Reserve Bank of St. Louis, 12 September 2018 (Updated), https://fred.stlouisfed.org/series/MEHOINUSA672N.

64 U.S. Bureau of the Census, *Income and Poverty in the United States: 2017.* Report Number P60-263. Washington, DC: September 2018, https://www.census.gov/content/dam/Census/library/publications/2018/demo/p60-263.pdf,

65 Hugo Bachega, "Homelessness in US: A deepening crisis on the streets." *BBC News.* 8 October 2018, https://www.bbc.com/news/world-us-canada-45442596.

66 Lynne Parramore, "America is Regressing into a Developing Nation for Most People." New York: Institute for New Economic Thinking (INET), 20 April 2017, https://www.ineteconomics.org/perspectives/blog/america-is-regressing-into-a-developing-nation-for-most-people.

67 Robert Reich, "Almost 80% of US workers live from paycheck to paycheck. Here's why." *The Guardian.* 29 July 2018, https://www.theguardian.com/commentisfree/2018/jul/29/us-economy-workers-paycheck-robert-reich.

68 Evan Comen, "Economic disparity: 10 States where the Middle class is left behind." *USA Today.* 5 March 2018, https://www.usatoday.com/story/money/economy/2018/03/01/economic-disparity-10-states-where-middle-class-being-left-behind/378376002/.

69 Jonathan Cribb et.al., *Living Standards, poverty, and inequality*

in the UK: 2018. London: Institute for Fiscal Studies, June 2018, https://www.ifs.org.uk/uploads/publications/comms/R129%20-%20 HBAI%20report%202017.pdf.

70 Rana Foroohar, "How hidden fees are making middle-class America poorer." *Financial Times*. 13 August 2018, https://www.ft.com/ content/86e8fb54-9c91-11e8-9702-5946bae86e6d.

71 Rana Foroohar, "The decline of America's middle classes." *Financial Times*. 21 June 2018, https://www.ft.com/content/a11fb8 04-7537-11e8-b6ad-3823e4384287.

72 Orazio Attanasio and Luigi Pistaferri, "Consumption Inequality." *Journal of Economic Perspectives*. Vol. 30, No. 2, Spring 2016: 1-5, 23, https://web.stanford.edu/~pista/JEP.pdf.

73 Nick Bunker, "A potentially new and rising concern: inflation inequality in the United States." Washington, DC: Washington Center for Equitable Growth. 14 March 2017, https://equitablegrowth. org/a-potentially-new-and-rising-concern-inflation-inequality-in-the-united-states/.

74 Chrystia Freeland, "The Rise of the New Global Elite." *The Atlantic*. January/February 2011, https://www.theatlantic.com/magazine/ archive/2011/01/the-rise-of-the-new-global-elite/308343/.

75 Alan B. Kreuger, "The Rise and Consequences of Inequality in the United States." Prepared remarks to the Center for American Progress (CAP). 12 January 2012, https://pages.wustl.edu/files/pages/imce/fazz/ ad_10_1_krueger.pdf.

76 Anthony Cilluffo, "Share of married Americans is falling, but they still pay most of the nation's income taxes." Washington, DC: Pew Research Center. 12 April 2017, http://www.pewresearch.org/fact-tank/2017/04/12/share-of-married-americans-is-falling-but-they-still-pay-most-of-the-nations-income-taxes/.

77 Foroohar, "How hidden fees are making middle-class America poorer."

78 Amanda Ripley, "Why is College in America so Expensive." *The Atlantic*. 11 September 2018, https://www.theatlantic.com/education/ archive/2018/09/why-is-college-so-expensive-in-america/569884/.

79 Annie Nova, "How student loans stop people from saving for retirement." *CNBC*. 23 May 2018, https://www.cnbc.com/2018/05/23/ how-your-student-loans-can-hurt-you-later-on-.html.

80 Eleanor Krause and Isabel V. Sawhill, "Seven reasons to worry about the American middle class." Washington, DC: Brookings Institution, 5 June 2018, https://www.brookings.edu/blog/social-

mobility-memos/2018/06/05/seven-reasons-to-worry-about-the-american-middle-class/.

81   Richard Florida, "The Geography of Middle Class Decline." *CityLab*. 15 November 2016, https://www.citylab.com/life/2016/11/the-geography-of-middle-class-decline/505769/.

82   Vincent Del Giudice and Wei Lu, "These Are the US Cities with the Fastest-Growing Wealth Gaps." *Bloomberg*. 19 April 2018, https://www.bloomberg.com/news/articles/2018-04-19/migration-from-pacific-coast-drives-boise-wealth-gains.

83   Ibid.

84   Mark Strassman, "Families earning $117,000 now qualify as 'low income' in California's Bay Area." *CBS News*. 26 June 2018, https://www.cbsnews.com/news/families-earning-117000-now-qualify-as-low-income-in-californias-bay-area/.

85   Andrew Van Dam, "The Strawberry Capital of the Word is the Early Death Capital of the US: lessons from a landmark dataset." *The Washington Post*. 14 September 2018, https://www.washingtonpost.com/business/2018/09/14/wrong-neighborhood-can-take-plus-years-off-your-life-average/?utm_term=.761253392614.

86   "Profile: Stilwell, Oklahoma." *DataUSA*. https://datausa.io/profile/geo/stilwell-ok/ [Accessed 11 November 2018].

87   Andrew Van Dam, "The Strawberry Capital of the Word is the Early Death Capital of the US: lessons from a landmark dataset."

88   Richard Reeves et. al., *Defining the Middle Class: Cash, credentials, or culture?*: 17-18.

89   Paul Kennedy, "The Rise of Vampire Capitalism (and not a slayer in sight)," in *Vampire Capitalism: Fractured Societies and Alternative Futures*. London: Palgrave Macmillan, 2017: 29-60.

90   Yossi Harpaz and Pablo Mateos, "Strategic Citizenship: negotiating membership in the age of dual nationality." *Journal of Ethnic and Migration Studies*. 20 March 2018: 1-15.

91   Freeland, "The Rise of the New Global Elite."

92   Olivia Carville, "The Super Rich of Silicon Valley Have a Doomsday Escape Plan in New Zealand." *Bloomberg*. 15 September 2018, https://www.bloomberg.com/features/2018-rich-new-zealand-doomsday-preppers/.

93   Frederick Solt, *Diversionary Nationalism: Economic Inequality and the Formation of National Pride*, LIS Working Paper Series, No. 495, Luxembourg Income Study (LIS), 2008, https://ideas.repec.org/p/lis/

liswps/495.html.

94 See USC Suzanne Dworak-Peck School of Social Work Research Note "Addressing the Pathways Toward Violent Extremism Among Military Service Members and Veterans." 11 September 2018, https://dworakpeck.usc.edu/news/addressing-the-pathways-toward-violent-extremism-among-military-service-members-and-veterans.

95 See Leo Shane III, "One in four troops sees white nationalism in the ranks." *Military Times*. 23 October 2017, https://www.militarytimes.com/news/pentagon-congress/2017/10/23/military-times-poll-one-in-four-troops-sees-white-nationalism-in-the-ranks/ and Leo Shane III, "Congressman wants answers on extremist activity in the military." *Army Times*. 7 May 2018, https://www.armytimes.com/news/pentagon-congress/2018/05/07/congressman-wants-answers-on-extremist-activity-in-the-military/.

96 Benjamin Luxenberg, "If inequality is our problem, military service is the answer." *Los Angeles Times*. 6 January 2015, http://www.latimes.com/nation/la-oe-luxenberg-military-service-as-asset-20150107-story.html.

97 Andrea Asoni and Tino Sanandaji, *Rich Man's War, Poor Man's Fight? Socioeconomic Representativeness in the Modern Military*. Stockholm, Sweden: Research Institute of Industrial Economics, IFN Working Paper No. 965, 2013, https://papers.ssrn.com/sol3/papers.cfm?abstract_id=2542143.

98 Jeffrey Kentor, Andrew Jorgenson, and Edward Kick, "The 'new' military and income inequality: A cross-national analysis." *Social Science Research*. Vol. 41, Iss. 3, May 2012: 514-526.

99 Roxanna Tiron and Robert Levinson, "Trump's Troops at Mexico Border Could Cost $10 million a Day." *Bloomberg Government*. 2 November 2018, https://about.bgov.com/blog/trumps-troops-mexico-border-10-million/.

100 Chris Davis, "Empire at War: The Effects of the War on Terrorism on the American Middle Class." *Small Wars Journal*. 23 April 2012, http://smallwarsjournal.com/blog/empire-at-war-the-effects-of-the-war-on-terrorism-on-the-american-middle-class.

101 George Sayers Bain, *Inequality and Instability*. Conference Paper, Munich Personal RePec Archive (MPRA). 14 May 2018, https://mpra.ub.uni-muenchen.de/86709/1/MPRA_paper_86709.pdf.

102 UN Secretary General, Antonio Guterres, "Address to the General Assembly." 25 September 2018, https://www.un.org/sg/en/content/sg/

speeches/2018-09-25/address-73rd-general-assembly.

103 Ramya Vijaya et. al., "Economic underpinnings of violent extremism: A cross country exploration of repeated survey data." *World Development*, Vol. 109, 2018: 411, https://ideas.repec.org/a/eee/wdevel/v109y2018icp401-412.html.

104 Eberhardt Karls, "Rich-poor gap and the risk of civil war." *Phys.org*. 4 June 2014, https://phys.org/news/2014-06-rich-poor-gap-civil-war.html.

105 Christopher Ingraham, "How rising inequality hurts everyone, even the rich." *The Washington Post*. 6 February 2018, http://wapo.st/2E81cxs?tid=ss_tw&utm_term=.b1e0d3a042da.

106 Matthew Stewart, "The 9.9 Percent is the New American Aristocracy." *The Atlantic*. June 2018, https://www.theatlantic.com/magazine/archive/2018/06/the-birth-of-a-new-american-aristocracy/559130/.

107 Walt Hunter, "The Story Behind the Poem on the Statue of Liberty." *The Atlantic*. 16 January 2018, https://www.theatlantic.com/entertainment/archive/2018/01/the-story-behind-the-poem-on-the-statue-of-liberty/550553/.

108 This includes hyper-rational behaviors to game economic systems. See "The real Goldfinger: The London banker who broke the world." *The Guardian*. 7 September 2018, https://www.theguardian.com/news/2018/sep/07/the-real-goldfinger-the-london-banker-who-broke-the-world.

109 Aakash Kumar, "As Regulators Make Predatory Lending Easier, Can Workers Break Free From Debt Trap Of Payday Loans?" *Forbes*. 12 May 2018, https://www.forbes.com/sites/aakashkumar/2018/05/12/as-regulators-make-predatory-lending-easier-can-workers-break-free-from-debt-trap-of-payday-loans/#2b71c6036a34, Robert J. Bunker and Pamela Ligouri Bunker, "Plutocratic Insurgency Note No. 7: Artificial Intelligence (AI) Pricing Software - Profit Optimization Beyond 'The Invisible Hand.'" *Small Wars Journal*. 7 January 2018, http://smallwarsjournal.com/jrnl/art/plutocratic-insurgency-note-no-7-artificial-intelligence-ai-pricing-software-profit, and Michael J. Coren, "Taking a cut of student's future paychecks has Silicon Valley investors funding education." *Quartz*. 9 February 2018, https://qz.com/1190860/taking-a-cut-of-students-future-paychecks-has-silicon-valley-investors-funding-education/.

110 Numerous articles have been written on this subject matter. See, for instance, Andrew Martin, "Old Debts That Won't Die." *The New York Times*. 30 July 2010, https://www.nytimes.com/2010/07/31/

business/31collect.html, Time Chen, "Student loans have become our modern-day debtors prisons." *USA Today*. 5 June 2018, https://www.usatoday.com/story/opinion/2018/06/05/student-loans-crisis-allow-bankruptcy-investigate-abuses-column/640460002/, and Sarah Berger, "1 in 10 Americans say they'll be in debt for the rest of their lives — reality is way worse." *CNBC News*. 5 September 2018, https://www.cnbc.com/2018/09/05/northwestern-mutual-how-many-americans-say-theyll-always-be-in-debt.html.

111 Percy Bysshe Shelly, "A Defence of Poetry." Unpublished, 1821. Later published in *Letters from Abroad, Translations and Fragments*. Vol. 1. London: Edward Moxon, 1840.

112 Associated Press, "Policies helping the rich get richer and the poor poorer, report says." *The Los Angeles Times*. 15 December 2017, http://www.latimes.com/business/la-fi-income-inequality-20171215-story.html.

113 Joel D. Joseph, "What's good for GM is not necessarily good for America." *The Hill*. 4 March 2016, https://thehill.com/blogs/congress-blog/economy-budget/271675-whats-good-for-gm-is-not-necessarily-good-for-america.

114 "Pittsburgh's Steel Mills." nd, www.brooklineconnection.com/history/Facts/Steel.html.

115 Jessica T. Mathews, "Power Shift." *Foreign Affairs*. January-February 1997, https://www.foreignaffairs.com/articles/1997-01-01/power-shift.

116 Such high salaries can quickly lead to predatory mentalities. This includes the use of U.S. Federal Reserve bail out funds during the financial crisis to pay out dividends and award employee bonuses. See Zach Carter, "Ten Years After The Financial Crisis, The Contagion Has Spread to Democracy Itself." *The Huffington Post*. 15 Septemebr 2018, https://www.huffingtonpost.com/entry/financial-crisis-10-years-later-ben-bernanke-hank-paulson-timothy-geithner_us_5b9d7dc8e4b04d32ebf92396.

117 Lauren Thomas, "As Wal-Mart blitzes Internet retail, debate rages over company's impact on US wages." *CNBC News*. 22 April 2017, https://www.cnbc.com/2017/04/20/wal-mart-still-front-and-center-of-debate-over-minimum-wages.html and Maxwell Strachan, "Walmart's Shiny New $11 Minimum Wage Isn't Really A Result Of The Tax Law." *The Huffington Post*. 12 January 2018, https://www.huffingtonpost.com/entry/walmart-minimum-wage_us_5a582a98e4b02cebbfda6799.

118 Bernard Marr, "How AI And Machine Learning Are Transforming Law

Firms And The Legal Sector." *Forbes*. 23 March 2018, https://www.forbes.com/sites/bernardmarr/2018/05/23/how-ai-and-machine-learning-are-transforming-law-firms-and-the-legal-sector/#64dd30dc32c3.

119 While the U.S. loses a significant amount to tax havens, the effects of offshore wealth has an even greater effect on inequality in other Western nations. See Annette Alstadsaeter, Niels Johannesen, and Gabriel Zucman, *Who Owns the Wealth in Tax Havens? Macro Evidence and Implications For Global Equality*, National Bureau of Economic Research (NBER), Working Paper No. 23805, 27 December 2017, https://gabriel-zucman.eu/files/AJZ2017b.pdf.

120 Gabriel Zucman, "How Corporations and the Wealthy Avoid Taxes (and How to Stop Them)." *The New York Times*. 10 November 2017, https://www.nytimes.com/interactive/2017/11/10/opinion/gabriel-zucman-paradise-papers-tax-evasion.html.

121 Ibid.

122 Edgar L. Feige and Richard J. Cebula, "America's Underground Economy: Measuring the Size, Growth and Determinants of Income Tax Evasion in the U.S." *Crime, Law and Social Change*. Vol. 57., Iss. 3, April 2012: 18, https://papers.ssrn.com/sol3/papers.cfm?abstract_id=2735051.

123 For an example of this phenomena taking place in Europe, see Bradley Hope, Drew Hinshaw, and Patricia Kowsmann, "How One Stubborn Banker Exposed a $200 Billion Russian Money-Laundering Scandal." *The Wall Street Journal*. 23 October 2018, https://www.wsj.com/articles/how-one-stubborn-banker-exposed-a-200-billion-russian-money-laundering-scandal-1540307327.

124 Jeremy Burke, "Here's where you can legally consume marijuana in the US in 2018." *Business Insider*. 17 October 2018, https://www.businessinsider.com/where-can-you-can-legally-smoke-weed-2018-1.

125 Stephen Hawkins et.al., *Hidden Tribes: A Study of America's Polarized Landscape*. New York: More in Common, October 2018, https://www.moreincommon.com/hidden-tribes/.

126 Ibid: 19.

127 Paul Waldman, "Saudi Arabia is putting money in Trump's pocket. Is that shaping U.S. policy?" *The Washington Post*. 16 October 2018, https://www.washingtonpost.com/blogs/plum-line/wp/2018/10/16/saudi-arabia-is-putting-money-in-trumps-pocket-is-that-shaping-u-s-policy/?utm_term=.0d8114b895b7 and Adam Whithall, "Donald

Trump says US is becoming a 'one party system.'" *The Independent*. 28 February 2017, https://www.independent.co.uk/news/world/americas/donald-trump-us-congress-address-republicans-democrats-one-party-system-a7603521.html.

128 Zach Carter, "Ten Years After the Financial Crisis, The Contagion Has Spread to Democracy Itself." *The Huffington Post*. 15 September 2018, https://www.huffingtonpost.com/entry/financial-crisis-10-years-later-ben-bernanke-hank-paulson-timothy-geithner_us_5b9d7dc8e4b04d32ebf92396.

129 See, for instance, Daniel Golden, "Many Colleges Bend Rules to Admit Elite Students." *The Wall Street Journal*. 20 February 2003, http://online.wsj.com/public/resources/documents/Polk_Rich_Applicants.htm and Jake New, "What Happens on Campus Stays on Campus?" *Inside Higher Education*. 27 February 2015, https://www.insidehighered.com/news/2015/02/27/how-institutions-handle-drug-violations-varies-greatly.

130 One law firm goes so far as to advertise outcomes for the rich. See Lance Fletcher, "After Arrest, the Rich Can Buy the Outcome they Need." *Criminal Defense Blog*. 4 February 2017, http://www.lawfletcher.com/Criminal-Defense-Blog/2017/February/After-Arrest-the-Rich-Can-Buy-the-Outcome-they-N.aspx. This impunity is representative of the broader trend of 'affluenza' taking place. Jessica Luther, "Affluenza: the latest excuse for the wealthy to do whatever they want." *The Guardian*. 15 Decemebr 2013, https://www.theguardian.com/commentisfree/2013/dec/15/affluenza-texas-dui-ethan-couch.

131 Josh Silver, "Partisan Gerrymandering Must End." *The Huffington Post*. 6 September 2017, https://www.huffingtonpost.com/entry/partisan-gerrymandering-must-end_us_59b007e2e4b0b5e53102b1e1, German Lopez, "Southern states have closed down at least 868 polling places for the 2016 election." *Vox*. 4 November 2016, https://www.vox.com/policy-and-politics/2016/11/4/13501120/vote-polling-places-election-2016, Jane C. Timm, "Voter purge frenzy after federal protections lifted, new report says." *NBC News*. 20 July 2018, https://www.nbcnews.com/politics/politics-news/voter-roll-purges-surged-after-changes-voting-rights-act-new-n893056, and Laura Strickler, "White House moves to replace Interior Department IG amid probe of Secretary Ryan Zinke." *NBC News*. 16 October 2018, https://www.nbcnews.com/politics/donald-trump/white-house-moves-replace-interior-department-ig-amid-probe-secretary-n920741.

132 Ben Tarnoff, "How privatization could spell the end of democracy." *The Guardian*. 21 June 2017, https://www.theguardian.com/technology/2017/jun/21/privatizing-public-services-trump-democracy. Such privatization further eliminates middle class jobs—see Timothy Noah, "How privatizing government hollowed out the middle class." *MSNBC*. 3 June 2014, http://www.msnbc.com/msnbc/government-privatization-hurts-middle-class.

133 Natalie Kitroeff, "Unemployment Rate Hits 3.9%, a Rare Low, as Job Market Becomes More Competitive." *The New York Times*. 4 May 2018, https://www.nytimes.com/2018/05/04/business/economy/jobs-report.html and Aimee Picchi, "America's job problem: Low wage work is growing fastest." *CBS News*. 4 August 2017, https://www.cbsnews.com/news/americas-job-problem-low-wage-work-is-growing-fastest/. See also Jeff Faux, *The Servant Economy: Where America's Elite is Sending the Middle Class*. New York: Wiley, 2012.

134 Richard Luscombe, "Life expectancy gap between rich and poor US regions is 'more than 20 years.'" *The Guardian*. 8 May 2017, https://www.theguardian.com/inequality/2017/may/08/life-expectancy-gap-rich-poor-us-regions-more-than-20-years.

135 Ibid.

136 Amy Fleming, "Heat: the next big inequality issue." *The Guardian*. 13 August 2018, https://www.theguardian.com/cities/2018/aug/13/heat-next-big-inequality-issue-heatwaves-world.

137 Isaiah Bollinger, "The Death of the Small Business." *The Trellis Blog*. 23 March 2017, https://trellis.co/blog/death-small-business/.

138 Brandon Smith, "4 Signs American Entrepreneurship Is Headed Towards An Ice Age." *Entrepreneur's Handbook*. 13 July 2017, https://entrepreneurshandbook.co/4-reasons-why-american-entrepreneurship-is-headed-towards-an-ice-age-3c46a80fd26 and J.D. Harrison, "The decline of American entrepreneurship — in five charts." *The Washington Post*. 12 February 2015, https://www.washingtonpost.com/news/on-small-business/wp/2015/02/12/the-decline-of-american-entrepreneurship-in-five-charts/?utm_term=.70d46e035afc.

139 Robert J. Bunker and Pamela Ligouri Bunker, "Plutocratic Insurgency Note No. 3: No Shoring: Job Obsolescence Via Artificial Intelligence (AI) and Robotics." *Small Wars Journal*. 22 Feburary 2017, http://smallwarsjournal.com/jrnl/art/plutocratic-insurgency-note-no-3-no-shoring-job-obsolescence-via-artificial-intelligence-ai.

140 "Chicago School." *Investopedia*. https://www.investopedia.com/

terms/c/chicago_school.asp.

141 It is increasingly difficult to have bi-partisan compromise when leading politicians make jokes about locking up their opponents or having their constituents mob political opponents in public places such as restaurants. This is the kind of rhetoric one would expect to see with authoritarian regimes where opposing candidates are harassed, threatened, imprisoned, tortured, and ultimately killed. See, for instance, Sara Boboltz, "Ted Cruz Jokes Beto O'Rouke Can Share A Prison Cell With Hillary Clinton." *The Huffington Post*. 24 October 2018, https://www.huffingtonpost.com/entry/ted-cruz-jokes-beto-orourke-c...h-hillary-clinton_us_5bd07373e4b0a8f17ef2c205?ncid=APPLENEWS00001, Jamie Ehrlich, "Maxine Waters encourages supporters to harass Trump administration officials." *CNN*. 25 June 2018, https://www.cnn.com/2018/06/25/politics/maxine-waters-trump-officials/index.html, Chris Sommerfeldt, "President Trump threatens California Rep. Maxine Waters in response to her rebuke of his administration." *AOL*. 25 June 2018, https://www.aol.com/article/news/2018/06/25/president-trump-threatens-california-rep-maxine-waters-in-response-to-her-rebuke-of-his-administration/23467564/.

142 See for example Daniella Greenbaum, "Democrats need to choose: Are they the party of Alexandria Ocasio-Cortez or the party of Michael Bloomberg?" *Business Insider*. 27 June 2018, John Fund, "Democrats Are Dumping Moderates." *The National Review*. 15 July 2018, https://www.nationalreview.com/2018/07/democrats-dump-moderates-move-to-far-left/, Erica Werner and Thomas Beaumont, "Unhappy Moderate Republicans Are Leaving Congress, Complicating 2018 for GOP." *NBC Washington*. 12 September 2017, https://www.nbcwashington.com/news/politics/Unhappy-Moderate-Republicans-Leaving-Congress-443936383.html, and Tom Nichols, "Why I'm Leaving the Republican Party." *The Atlantic*. 7 October 2018, https://www.theatlantic.com/ideas/archive/2018/10/tom-nichols-why-im-leaving-republican-party/572419/. See also Sunil Ahuja, *Congress Behaving Badly: The Rise of Partisanship and Incivility and the Death of Public Trust*. Westport, Ct: Praeger Publishers, 2008.

143 Jeffrey M. Jones, "Americans' Identification as Independents Back Up in 2017." *Gallup*. 8 January 2018, https://news.gallup.com/poll/225056/americans-identification-independents-back-2017.aspx.

144 For thinking on why independents are 'independent' and their 3rd party potentials, see Philip Bump, "Why political independents are political

independents." *The Washington Post.* 30 March 2018, https://www.washingtonpost.com/news/politics/wp/2018/03/30/why-political-independents-are-political-independents/?utm_term=.9769a4bfc9aa.

145 A Greek tragic dramatist who lived from 525 BC to 456 BC.

146 Jim Garamone, "Eucom Commander Discusses Counteracting Russian Disinformation." *DoD News.* U.S. Department of Defense. 16 March 2018, https://dod.defense.gov/News/Article/Article/1468525/eucom-commander-discusses-counteracting-russian-disinformation/, Keir Giles, "Countering Russian Information Operations in the Age of Social Media." Council on Foreign Relations. 21 November 2017, https://www.cfr.org/report/countering-russian-information-operations-age-social-media, Associated Press, "China takes aim at heartland famers with propaganda push." *Washington Examiner.* 20 October 2018, https://www.washingtonexaminer.com/news/china-takes-aim-at-heartland-famers-with-propaganda-push, and Marshall Sahlins, "Confucius Institutes: Academic Malware and Cold Warfare." *The Chronicle of Higher Education.* 26 July 2018, https://www.insidehighered.com/views/2018/07/26/confucius-institutes-function-propaganda-arms-chinese-government-opinion.

147 Nathan Kelly and Peter Enns, "Inequality and the Dynamics of Public Opinion: The Self-Reinforcing Link Between Economic Inequality and Mass Preferences." *American Journal of Political Science.* Vol. 54, No. 4, October 2010: 867, 869.

148 See Frederick Solt and Veli-Matti Ritakallio, *Economic inequality and democratic political engagement.* LIS Working Paper Series No. 385, Luxembourg Income Study (LIS), 2004, https://www.econstor.eu/bitstream/10419/95580/1/472645862.pdf.

149 Corporate executives have merged with the present presidential administration as the next round of governance evolution in the U.S. See Sarah Chayes, "Kleptocracy in America." *Foreign Affairs.* September/October 2017, 142-150.

150 "Public Corruption." Federal Bureau of Investigation. nd, https://archives.fbi.gov/archives/about-us/ten-years-after-the-fbi-since-9-11/just-the-facts-1/public-corruption-1. These have also been termed 'public corruption task forces.' See "FBI, This Week: The Tarnished Badge Task Force." Federal Bureau of Investigation. 14 December 2017, https://www.fbi.gov/audio-repository/ftw-podcast-tarnished-badge-task-force-121417.mp3/view.

151 Jack Goldsmith, "The Cost of Trump's Attacks on the FBI." *The*

Atlantic. 4 December 2017, https://www.theatlantic.com/politics/archive/2017/12/the-high-price-of-sessionss-failure-to-defend-the-justice-department/547382/, Eric Lichtblau, "The FBI Is in Crisis. It's Worse Than You Think." *Time.* 3 May 2018, http://time.com/5264153/the-fbi-is-in-crisis-and-america-is-paying-the-price/, and Lawrence Hurley, "Chaos grips Senate hearing on Trump Supreme Court pick Kavanaugh." *Reuters.* 4 September 2018, https://www.reuters.com/article/us-usa-court-kavanaugh/chaos-grips-senate-hearing-on-trump-supreme-court-pick-kavanaugh-idUSKCN1LK0YB.

152 Kimberly Amadeo, "Interest on the National Debt and How It Affects You." *The Balance.* 19 March 2018, https://www.thebalance.com/interest-on-the-national-debt-4119024.

153 Ibid.

154 Michael Hiltzik, "Mitch McConnell says it out loud: Republicans are gunning for Social Security, Medicare and Obamacare next." *The Los Angeles Times.* 19 October 2018, http://www.latimes.com/business/hiltzik/la-fi-hiltzik-mcconnell-social-security-20181019-story.html and John Wasik, "How GOP Plan To Gut Social Security, Medicare Stokes Americans' Biggest Fear." *Forbes.* 22 October 2018, https://www.forbes.com/sites/johnwasik/2018/10/22/how-gop-plan-to-gut-social-security-medicare-stokes-americans-biggest-fear/#3aa9344576a7.

155 The private prison industry has taken a bit of a hit but is now on the upswing again. See Aimee Picchi, "One winner under Trump: The private prison industry." *CBS News.* 21 February 2018, https://www.cbsnews.com/news/one-winner-under-trump-the-private-prison-industry/ and Zusha Elinson, "Trump's Immigrant-Detention Plans Benefit Private Prison Operators." *The Wall Street Journal.* 2 July 2018, https://www.wsj.com/articles/trumps-immigrant-detention-plans-benefit-these-companies-1530523800.

156 See, for example, Suzanne Mettler, "How the G.I. Bill Built the Middle Class," a synopsis of her book *Soldiers to Citizens: The G.I. Bill and the Making of the Greatest Generation.* Oxford: Oxford University Press, 2005, https://scholars.org/sites/scholars/files/ssn_key_findings_mettler_on_gi_bill.pdf.

157 "On War, by U.S General Smedley Butler (1933)." http://quaker.org/legacy/co/Writings/SmedleyButler.htm.

158 Lewis L. Gould, *The Presidency of Theodore Roosevelt.* Lawrence, KS: University of Kansas Press, 2011 and Michael McGerr, *A Fierce Discontent: The Rise and Fall of the Progressive Movement in America.*

New York: Oxford University Press, 2005. For a new and more nuanced perspective on 'trust busting,' refer to Gerard Helferich, *An Unlikely Trust: Theodore Roosevelt, J.P. Morgan, and the Improbable Partnership That Remade American Business.* Guilford, CT: Lyons Press, 2018.

159 For an early work on this paradigm, see T. Lindsay Moore, "The Structure of War: Early Fourth Epoch War Research." *Small Wars & Insurgency.* Vol 13, Iss. 2, 2002: 159-170, https://www.tandfonline.com/doi/abs/10.1080/09592310208559189.

160 Hedley Bull, *The Anarchical Society: A Study of Order in World Politics.* New York: Columbia University Press, 1977; Martin van Creveld, *The Transformation of War.* New York: The Free Press, 1991; Phillip Bobbitt, *The Shield of Achilles: War, Peace, and the Course of History.* New York: Anchor Books, 2002; and Nils Gilman, Jesse Goldhammer, and Steven Weber, Eds., *Deviant Globalization: Black Market Economy in the 21ˢᵗ Century.* New York: Continuum, 2011.

161 See Robert J. Bunker and Pamela Ligouri Bunker, "Dark Renaissance—crime, corruption, and global class warfare." Robert J. Bunker and Pamela Ligouri Bunker, Eds., *Global Criminal and Sovereign Free Economies and the Demise of the Western Democracies: Dark Renaissance.* New York: Routledge, 2015: 2-6.

162 For an understanding of these battlespace dynamics, see Robert J. Bunker and Charles "Sid" Heal, Eds., *Fifth Dimensional Operations: Space-Time-Cyber Dimensionality in Conflict and War—A Terrorism Research Center Book.* Bloomington, IA: iUniverse, 2014.

163 An earlier SSI monograph analyzed weapons systems life cycles related to the knight, the battleship, and the tank and then discussed the implications this held for armed robotic systems. Within the context of this table, the knight exists in the Medieval era, the battleship and tank exist in the Modern era, and the armed robotic system exists within the Post-Modern era. See Robert J. Bunker, *Armed Robotic Systems Emergence: Weapons Systems Life Cycles Analysis and New Strategic Realities.* Carlisle, PA: Strategic Studies Institute, U.S. Army War College, 14 November 2017, https://ssi.armywarcollege.edu/pubs/display.cfm?pubID=1368.

164 The pivotal issue, of course, is that with robots—rather than humans—engaging in the labor of production, how can humans then earn a wage to be able to purchase agricultural and manufactured products. Speculation presently exists concerning what a post-capitalist economy may look like. An early work discussing the knowledge economy

component of such a future is Peter F. Drucker, *Post-Capitalist Society*. New York: HarperBusiness, 1993. Distant musings about such an automated future dystopia can be found in Kurt Vonnegut Jr.'s *Player Piano: America in the Coming Age of Electronics*. New York: Charles Scribner's Sons, 1952.

165 Early perceptions related to this projected class structure can be found in Robert J. Bunker, "Enhanced and Unenhanced Humans: The Social Classes of a Dark Renaissance." *Crime & Justice International Online*. Office of International Criminal Justice, University of Chicago at Illinois. 3 September 1999: 1-5.

166 See, for instance, Patrick Tucker, "Defense Intel Chief Worried About Chinese 'Integration of Human and Machines.'" *Defense One*. 10 October 2018, https://www.defenseone.com/technology/2018/10/defense-intel-chief-worried-about-chinese-integration-human-and-machines/151904/?oref=d-river and Michael Joseph Gross, "The Pentagon's Push to Program Soldiers' Brains." *Defense One*. 13 October 2018, https://www.defenseone.com/ideas/2018/10/pentagons-push-program-soldiers-brains/151943/?oref=d-river. For an even earlier work, see Steven Metz, "How Far Can the U.S. Military Go to Building a Technology-Enhanced 'Super Soldier'?" *World Politics Review*. 23 September 2016, https://www.worldpoliticsreview.com/articles/19992/how-far-can-the-u-s-military-go-to-building-a-technology-enhanced-super-soldier.

167 Sarju Sing Rai, "Global Explosion of Slums: The Next Biggest Planetary Health Challenge." *Medium*. 22 April 2017, https://medium.com/amplify/global-explosion-of-slums-the-next-biggest-planetary-health-challenge-49424f27ba16. For background on this issue, see Mike Davis, *Planet of Slums*. London: Verso, 2007.

168 Other candidate dates for the demarcation into the Modern era include the French artillery train unleashed upon Italy by Charles VIII in 1494 and the Treaty of Westphalia in 1648 securing the sovereign territorial and internal domestic rights of emergent nation-states.

169 *Fund for Peace 2018 Fragile States Index*. Washington, DC: 24 April 2018, http://fundforpeace.org/fsi/wp-content/uploads/2018/04/951181805-Fragile-States-Index-Annual-Report-2018.pdf.

170 While a U.S. 'Space Force' has been proposed, humanity is still far off from colonizing the moon or the planets within our solar system. See Claudette Roulo, "Space Force to Become Sixth Branch of Armed Forces." U.S. Department of Defense. 9 August 2018, https://dod.defense.gov/

News/Article/Article/1598071/space-force-to-become-sixth-branch-of-armed-forces/.

171 Initial examples of the decisive demonstration of a new form of energy on the battlefield (e.g. animal and mechanical derived; cavalry and firearm based weaponry, respectively) and the resulting demise of the defender of the earlier civilizational order (e.g. the Roman legionnaire and the Medieval knight) have proven to be too premature in their timing (and potentially too academic) to make a compelling argument concerning this historical process of cyclical state form deconstruction. See Robert J. Bunker, "Epochal Change: War Over Social and Political Organization." *Parameters*. Summer 1997: 15-25, http://strategicstudiesinstitute.army.mil/pubs/parameters/Articles/97summer/bunker.htm and T. Lindsay Moore, "The Structure of War: Early Fourth Epoch War Research."

172 Steven Metz, *The Future of Insurgency*. Carlisle, PA: Strategic Studies Institute, U.S Army War College, 10 December 1993, https://ssi.armywarcollege.edu/pubs/display.cfm?pubID=344.

173 Ibid: 5.

174 Ibid: 5, 15-16.

175 John P. Sullivan and Adam Elkus, "State of Siege: Mexico's Criminal Insurgency." *Small Wars Journal*. 12 August 2008, http://smallwarsjournal.com/blog/journal/docs-temp/84-sullivan.pdf.

176 Robert J. Bunker, "Plutocratic Insurgency." *Small Wars Journal*. 5 September 2012, http://smallwarsjournal.com/blog/plutocratic-insurgency.

177 For an overview and analysis of post-Cold War insurgency forms, see Robert J. Bunker, *Old and New Insurgency Forms*, Carlisle, PA: Strategic Studies Institute, U.S Army War College, 15 March 2016, https://ssi.armywarcollege.edu/pubs/display.cfm?pubID=1313.

178 This initial overview is partially adapted from Robert J. Bunker, "Op-Ed: Not Your Grandfather's Insurgency — Criminal, Spiritual, and Plutocratic." Strategic Insights. Carlisle, PA: Strategic Studies Institute, U.S Army War College, 20 February 2014, https://ssi.armywarcollege.edu/index.cfm/articles//Not-Your-Grandfathers-Insurgency-Criminal-Spiritual-and-Plutocratic/2014/02/20.

179 John P. Sullivan, *From Drug Wars to Criminal Insurgency: Mexican Cartels, Criminal Enclaves and Criminal Insurgency in Mexico and Central America. Implications for Global Security*. MSH-WP- 2012-09. 2011. Paris: Archive ouverte en Sciences de l'Homme et de la

Société (HAL), 4 August 2012: 7-8, https://halshs.archives-ouvertes. fr/halshs-00694083.

180 Research products include Robert J. Bunker, Ed., *Criminal Insurgencies in Mexico and the Americas*. London: Routledge, 2013 and the six edited anthologies derived from *Small Wars Journal—El Centro* (http://smallwarsjournal.com/elcentro/about-el-centro) articles; John P. Sullivan and Robert J. Bunker, *Mexico's Criminal Insurgency*. Bloomington, IN: iUniverse, 2012 through John P. Sullivan and Robert J. Bunker, Eds., *The Rise of the Narcostate (Mafia States)*. Bloomington, IN: Xlibris, 2018. Additionally, Ioan Grillo has also acceded to the construct in his two works *El Narco: Inside Mexico's Criminal Insurgency*. New York: Bloomsbury Press, 2012 and *Gangster Warlords*. New York: Bloomsbury Press, 2017.

181 Partially adapted from Robert J. Bunker, "Op-Ed: Not Your Grandfather's Insurgency — Criminal, Spiritual, and Plutocratic."

182 For an overview of this research, see "Research Guide: Plutocratic Insurgency— The Gilded Age Redux ." *Small Wars Journal.* 15 March 2018, http://smallwarsjournal.com/jrnl/art/ research-guide-plutocratic-insurgency-gilded-age-redux.

183 Robert J. Bunker and Pamela Ligouri Bunker, "Plutocratic Insurgency Note No. 1: Eight Individuals are Now as Wealthy as the Poorest Half of the World." *Small Wars Journal.* 9 February 2017, http:// smallwarsjournal.com/jrnl/art/plutocratic-insurgency-note-no-1-eight-individuals-are-now-as-wealthy-as-the-poorest-half-o and Pamela Ligouri Bunker and Robert J. Bunker, "Plutocratic Insurgency Note No. 2: 69% of Americans Don't Even Have $1,000 in Savings." *Small Wars Journal.* 14 February 2017, http://smallwarsjournal.com/jrnl/art/ plutocratic-insurgency-note-no-2-69-of-americans-don't-even-have-1000-in-savings.

184 Robert J. Bunker, "Op-Ed: Not Your Grandfather's Insurgency — Criminal, Spiritual, and Plutocratic."

185 Nils Gilman, "The twin insurgency—facing plutocrats and criminals." Robert J. Bunker and Pamela Ligouri Bunker, Eds., *Global Criminal and Sovereign Free Economies and the Demise of the Western Democracies: Dark Renaissance*: xx-xxxvi.

186 Ibid: xxvii-xxviii.

187 Robert J. Bunker and Pamela Ligouri Bunker, "Introduction: Dark Renaissance—crime, corruption, and global class warfare": 2-11.

188 Niv Elis, "White House budget projects $1 trillion deficit in

2019." *The Hill*. 17 July 2018, https://thehill.com/homenews/administration/397445-white-house-budget-projects-1-trillion-deficit-in-2019, "U.S. Debt Clock." 15 October 2018, http://www.usdebtclock.org, and Robert J. Bunker, Nils Gilman, John P. Sullivan and Pamela Ligouri Bunker, "Plutocratic Insurgency Note No. 9: Tax Cuts and Jobs Act—Class Warfare 'Red Line' Crossed." *Small Wars Journal*. 11 January 2018, http://smallwarsjournal.com/jrnl/art/plutocratic-insurgency-note-no-9-tax-cuts-and-jobs-act-class-warfare-red-line-crossed.

189 The section entitled 'Autocratic States: The Future Evolution of Narco/Mafia States?' in the introduction to the new work *The Rise of the Narcostate (Mafia States)* discusses these new perceptions. See: li.

190 See the comments of Branko Milanovic, "The two insurgencies." *globalinequality*. 18 August 2016, http://glineq.blogspot.com/2016/08/the-two-insurgencies.html.

191 Sandra Weiss, "Narco cartels target politicians as Mexico's elections near." *Duetsche Welle*. 22 April 2018, https://www.dw.com/en/narco-cartels-target-politicians-as-mexicos-elections-near/a-43489100.

192 Adam Lusher, "At least 10,000 people died in Tiananmen Square massacre, secret British cable from the time alleged." *The Independent*. 23 December 2017, https://www.independent.co.uk/news/world/asia/tiananmen-square-massacre-death-toll-secret-cable-british-ambassador-1989-alan-donald-a8126461.html, Ben Westcott and Yong Xiong, "China legalizes Xinjiang 're-education camps' after denying they exist." *CNN*. 11 October 2018, https://www.cnn.com/2018/10/10/asia/xinjiang-china-reeducation-camps-intl/index.html, and *Orwell's Nightmare: China's Social Credit System*. Seoul, Korea: The Asan Institute for Policy Studies, 28 February 2017, http://en.asaninst.org/contents/orwells-nightmare-chinas-social-credit-system/.

193 Seth G. Jones and Patrick B. Johnson, "The Future of Insurgency." *Studies in Conflict & Terrorism*, Vol. 36, Iss. 1, 2013, p. 1.

194 Robert J. Bunker, *Old and New Insurgency Forms*: 50-52. Steven Metz as of the publication of that paper was skeptical that China would attempt to implement such an insurgency form directed at the U.S.

195 Ibid. China is viewing these policies as part of a containment strategy, see "China must prepare for US' containment." *Global Times*. 4 July 2018, http://www.globaltimes.cn/content/1109537.shtml and Christopher Scott, "US tariffs arecontainment: Beijing's message, fed by the White House." *Asia Times*. 5 September 2018, http://www.atimes.com/article/

us-tariffs-are-containment-beijings-message-fed-by-the-white-house/.

196 For Russian election hacking and U.S. consensus targeting via social media, see "Facebook removes 135 accounts linked to Russian troll farm." *Al Jazeera.* 4 April 2018, "Twelve Russians charged with US 2016 election hack." *BBC News.* 13 July 2018, https://www.bbc.com/news/world-us-canada-44825345, "Russia trolls 'spreading vaccination misinformation' to create discord." *BBC News.* 24 August 2018, and https://www.bbc.com/news/world-us-canada-45294192.

197 Demographics issues, however, still plague both states with Russian losing population due to Western sanctions and China facing an increasing aging population. Mark Lawrence Schrad, "Western Sanctions Are Shrinking Russia's Population." *Foreign Policy.* 19 October 2017, https://foreignpolicy.com/2017/10/19/western-sanctions-are-shrinking-russias-population/ and "China's Next Debt Bomb Is an Aging Population." *Bloomberg News.* 5 February 2018, https://www.bloomberg.com/news/articles/2018-02-05/china-s-next-debt-bomb-is-an-aging-population.

198 Robert J. Bunker, "Research Guide: Plutocratic Insurgency - The Gilded Age Redux." *Small Wars Journal.* 15 March 2018, http://smallwarsjournal.com/jrnl/art/research-guide-plutocratic-insurgency-gilded-age-redux. Originally published in Robert J. Bunker and Pamela Ligouri Bunker, Eds., *Global Criminal and Sovereign Free Economies and the Demise of the Western Democracies: Dark Renaissance*: 8.

199 A case in point is the U.S. invasion of Panama (Operation Just Cause) from December 1989 through January 1990 while under the dictatorship of Manuel Noriega.

200 Kai-Fu Lee, *AI-Superpowers: China, Silicon Valley, and the New World Order.* Boston: Houghton Mifflin Harcourt, 2018: 101-103.

201 David Lee, "The tactics of a Russian troll farm." *BBC News.* 16 February 2018, https://www.bbc.com/news/technology-43093390, David E. Sanger, "Russian Hackers Appear to Shift Focus to U.S. Power Grid." *The New York Times.* 27 July 2018, https://www.nytimes.com/2018/07/27/us/politics/russian-hackers-electric-grid-elections-.html, and Lily Hay Newman, "China Escalates Hacks Against the US as Trade Tensions Rise." *Wired.* 22 June 2018, https://www.wired.com/story/china-hacks-against-united-states/.

202 Adapted from Robert J. Bunker, *Old and New Insurgency Forms*: 54.

203 For related perceptions concerning the U.S. losing the institutional knowledge gained from almost 20 years of counterinsurgency lessons

learned, see Steven Metz, "The U.S. Is Again at Risk of Abandoning the Lessons of Counterinsurgency." *World Politics Review.* 9 November 2018, https://www.worldpoliticsreview.com/articles/26709/the-u-s-is-again-at-risk-of-abandoning-the-lessons-of-counterinsurgency.

204 For an example of scholarship in this area, see Phillip Bobbitt, *The Shield of Achilles: War, Peace, and the Course of History.* New York: Anchor Books, 2003. Three market-state forms—entrepreneurial, merchantile, and managerial—are proposed as follow-on variants to the modern nation-state. Also see John Robb, "Nation-states, Market-states, and Virtual-states." *Global Crime.* Vol. 7., Iss. 3-4., 2006. Published online 14 February 2007, https://www.tandfonline.com/doi/abs/10.1080/17440570601063864.

205 Katie Lange, "3rd Offset Strategy 101: What It Is, What the Tech Focuses Are." *DoDLive.* 30 March 2016, http://www.dodlive.mil/2016/03/30/3rd-offset-strategy-101-what-it-is-what-the-tech-focuses-are/.

206 The present U.S. defense budget is simply not economically sustainable. See Aaron Mehta, "It's official: DoD told to take cut with FY20 budget." *Defense News.* 26 October 2018, https://www.defensenews.com/pentagon/2018/10/26/its-official-dod-told-to-take-cut-with-fy20-budget/.

207 James A. Winnefeld Jr. and Amy Schafer, "Military is trending regional and 'all in the family.' We need more diversity." *USA Today.* 29 May 2017, https://www.usatoday.com/story/opinion/2017/05/29/military-has-too-many-troops-same-families-regions-column/102026774/.

208 Amy Schafer, "The Warrior Caste." *Slate.* 2 August 2017, https://slate.com/news-and-politics/2017/08/the-warrior-caste-of-military-families-that-fight-americas-wars.html.

209 For background on the fielding of armed droids and drones, see Robert J. Bunker, *Armed Robotic Systems Emergence: Weapons Systems Life Cycles Analysis and New Strategic Realities.* Carlisle, PA: Strategic Studies Institute, U.S. Army War College, 14 November 2017, https://ssi.armywarcollege.edu/pubs/display.cfm?pubID=1368.

210 Marissa Fessenden, "How 1960s Mouse Utopias Led to Grim Predictions for Future of Humanity." *Smithsonian.* 26 February 2015, https://www.smithsonianmag.com/smart-news/how-mouse-utopias-1960s-led-grim-predictions-humans-180954423/.

211 Let us not forget that increasingly the 'Red army' sided with the proletariat against the aristocracy and bourgeoisie during the Russian revolution which precipitated decades of totalitarian rule and tens of

millions of deaths during the ensuing purges that took place within that nation.

212 Kai-Fu Lee, *AI-Superpowers: China, Silicon Valley, and the New World Order*: 164.

213 See, for instance, Andy Stern, *Raising the Floor: How a Universal Basic Income Can Renew Our Economy and Rebuild the American Dream*. New York: PublicAffairs, 2016 and Philippe Van Parijs and Yannick Vanderborght, *Basic Income: A Radical Proposal for a Free Society and a Sane Economy*. Harvard: Harvard University Press, 2017.

214 Kai-Fu Lee, *AI-Superpowers: China, Silicon Valley, and the New World Order*: 197-225. Such 'social cohesion enhancing' employment would specifically represent 'societal bond-relationship protection'—think of this as the strategic equivalent of disruptive defense to operational level destructive defense (i.e. force protection).

215 Thomas F. Homer-Dixon, *Environment, Scarcity, and Violence*. Princeton: Princeton University Press, 1999, Robert Kaplan, *The Coming Anarchy: Shattering the Dreams of the Post Cold War*. New York: Vintage, 2001, Noreena Hertz, *The Silent Takeover: Global Capitalism and the Death of Democracy*. New York: The Free Press, 2001, Mike Davis, *Planet of Slums*. New York: Verso, 2006, and Naomi Klein, *The Shock Doctrine: The Rise of Disaster Capitalism*. New York: Metropolitan Books, 2006.

216 Even in the case of the recent California wildfires, the elite have commoditized the public good of fire fighting and have hired their own private fire fighters. See Robert Raymond, "As California's Wildfires Raged, The Ultra-Rich Hired Private Firefighters." *The Huffington Post*. 15 November 2018, https://www.huffingtonpost.com/entry/california-wildfires-neoliberalism-climate-change_us_5bec0d2ce4b0caeec2c012a0.

217 It should be noted that those nationals and foreign residents residing inside of such states that are representative of the global elite (e.g. the richest 1%-.01%) and functioning very much as extra-sovereign citizens will of course not require such assistance—they long ago commoditized such basic needs as personal security, access to food, water, and air conditioning, and will have private business entities servicing their requirements.

218 See Walter Scheidel, *The Great Leveler: Violence and the History of Inequality from the Stone Age to the Twenty-First Century*. Princeton: Princeton University Press, 2017 and Walter Scheidel, "The Only

Thing, Historically, That's Curbed Inequality: Catastrophe." *The Atlantic*. 21 February 2017, https://www.theatlantic.com/business/archive/2017/02/scheidel-great-leveler-inequality-violence/517164/.

219 While the concept of a police-like state emerging in the U.S. derived from growing levels of authoritarianism may sound ludicrous (and even paranoia driven), it must now at least be taken into consideration from a futures perspective given the changing nature of global based capitalism. China is actively utilizing technologies of social control domestically with the implementation of its AI and facial technology driven 'social credit system' and writings by U.S. scholars related concerns over 'digital capitalism and [the] global police state' are now being produced. See, for instance, Megan Palin, "Big Brother: China's chilling dictatorship moves to introduce scorecards to control everyone." *News AU*. 19 September 2018, https://www.news.com.au/technology/online/big-brother-chinas-chilling-dictatorship-moves-to-introduce-scorecards-to-control-everyone/news-story/6c821cbf15378ab0d3eeb3ec3dc98abf and William I. Robinson, "The next economic crisis: digital capitalism and global police state." *Race & Class*. Vol. 60., Iss. 1., 4 May 2018: 1-16. Additionally, sovereign states when they are under increasing institutional pressure—due to increased levels of internal conflict—will overly centralize themselves and limit individual freedoms in order to promote collective security needs; security needs ultimately benefiting the elites in society and the status quo.